"The Church of Stop Shopping is in the vanguard of a new movement that challenges this consumer society that is killing our planet." — Mike Roselle, Climate Ground Zero and Coal River Mountain Watch

"Ssssh, listen . . . let the Church of Stop Shopping exorcise your fear, doubt and burnout, and join the Earthalujah Revolution!" — Jess Worth, BP or not BP?

"This call to action is at once sobering and encouraging. We have fucked up really badly, but the ability to see it—is the first and hardest step toward fixing it." — Douglas Rushkoff, author of *Throwing Rocks at the Google Bus*

"Reverend Billy's ALL IN! bodies and voices . . . not just clicks and posts, for this small village we call Earth. Preach On!" — Obang Metho, Solidarity Movement for a New Ethiopia

"The Stop Shoppers pack a whoop." — Roberto Sifuentes, La Pocha Nostra

"In between satire and silence, there is a space of penetrating reckoning for all vibrations that flow counter to the balance of Nature. And from this dynamic and tricky space, the Honorable Reverend and his Holified Choir will shout, sing and sermonize a soul-bound love message of Truthalujah!" John Sims, *The AfroDixie Remixes*

"He seems to be writing while his actions are going on, like he can write while he's hand-cuffed." — Benny Zable, The Nimbin Environment Centre, NSW Australia

"Reverend Talen is a warrior whose aim it is to wake the sleeping to the realities of climate change. He is guided by a higher power and fueled by love." — Clayton Thomas-Muller, member of the Mathais Colomb Cree Nation (Pukatawagan), Manitoba

"*The Earth Wants You* takes readers deep inside the heart, mind and balls of the activist–artist. Reverend Billy rocks hard!" — Annie Sprinkle, artist, ecosexual sexecologist

"He was a comic act. Now he's evolved into a man compulsively challenging the true extent of the right to protest." — Anohni, creator of the song "4 Degrees"

"I had a dream about the Reverend Billy last night. He came to Harvard Divinity School. People were distraught that no one had authorized him as a reverend to preach, and yet he preached." — Tim DeChristopher, Peaceful Uprising

"The Church of Stop Shopping helps us ready ourselves for the times ahead by finding solace in the persistent force field of living beings." — Severine von Tscharner Fleming, The Greenhorns

"Reverend Billy will have you raising your hands in Hallelujah while the Earth's plight brings you to your knees."— Zen Honeycutt, Moms Across America

"This is a movement that you hold in your hands, which you will then feed back to the wind, to the fire and the water." — Leah Borromeo, *The Cotton Film: Dirty White Gold*

"This is a new Psalm for the Earth, for her human and other-than-human inhabitants." —Beth Stephens, ecosexual artist, professor

"The Reverend reminds us that we are complicit in the delusion that we are somehow separate from the evolutionary process of Mother Earth."— Alnoor Ladha, The Rules

"This is a kaleidoscopic journey, from disobedient grandma's fighting fracking to rebellious choirs against police racism, from profound animistic prayers on ecological collapse to complex political critiques of the NGO sector."— John Jordan, Laboratoire d'Imagination Insurrectionnelle

"He's hysterically serious."— Andy Shallal, Busboys and Poets

"Billy, Savi and the choir have love and optimistic humor, and they don't give up on people." — David LaChapelle, surrealist, photographer

"Out of the murky and uncertain darkness of climate chaos strides Reverend Billy and his posse of radical possibilitarians, shouting and singing and praising the light that binds us together in a common struggle for LIFE ITSELF. I see it! I see the light! Lifealujah!" — Mark Read, The Illuminator

"Earthalujah! Earthalujah!"— Amanda Starbuck, Rainforest Action Network

THE EARTH WANTS YOU

Reverend Billy Talen

City Lights Books | San Francisco

Cover photo © John Quilty
Photos on pp. 19, 47-48 and 73-74 © Erik McGregor
Photo on p. 101 © John Quilty
Photo on p. 118 © Kevin Ryan

Library of Congress Cataloging-in-Publication Data
Names: Talen, William, author.
Title: The earth wants you / Reverend Billy Talen.
Description: San Francisco : City Lights Publishers, [2016]
Identifiers: LCCN 2015049238| ISBN 9780872867079 (paperback) | ISBN
  9780872867086 (ebook)
Subjects: LCSH: Environmentalism. | Environmental responsibility. |
  Sustainable development. | Political participation. | BISAC: POLITICAL
  SCIENCE / Civics & Citizenship. | PERFORMING ARTS / Theater / General. |
  NATURE / Environmental Conservation & Protection.
Classification: LCC GE195 .T34 2016 | DDC 363.7—dc23
LC record available at http://lccn.loc.gov/2015049238

City Lights Books are published at the City Lights Bookstore
261 Columbus Avenue, San Francisco, CA 94133
www.citylights.com

for Savi and Lena

Our old ones were talking about this. And they were saying that there is coming a time when the Earth will rise up because she needs to cleanse herself. And it could go one of two ways. The Earth rises up and then the people rise up with her. Or the Earth rises up. And the people don't. And then they fall away. And they are no longer here.

— *prophecy recounted by Debra White Plume of the Lakota Nation, and retold at Occupy Wall Street by Kandi Mossett of the Mandan, Hidatsa and Arikara people*

CONTENTS

INTRODUCTION

LIFE IN THESE TIMES IS LIKE being trapped in a Tower of Babel that echoes with pleas for help. Emails and texts and self-addressed stamped envelopes, algorithmic requests for donations: *Help us save the children! Save the world! Save me!* One of the pleas is especially impressive, dramatized by really amazing special effects, with trillion-dollar budgets and the tragic collateral damage of countless lives lost to storms, floods, droughts and fires. Oh, I see . . . it's a message from the Earth itself.

Let's entertain the idea that the Earth wants to communicate directly with us humans. That's a little hard to take, isn't it? Who thinks of the Earth as having needs, moods, health problems, and even some kind of strategic intelligence? The Earth communicates? The Earth speaks?

If the Earth is saying something with its climate chaos and extinction wave, what is it? Whatever it might be, the consumer culture of the United States will have none of it. Public figures refuse to repeat what the bad weather is saying. At one point recently more than half of the counties in the country were in federally certified states of emergency, and yet the American media machine was so silent on the matter that you had to ask yourself, "Who's the censor?" If the Earth is indeed speaking to us, we've chosen to demote that talk into tabloid scandal, teleprompter speechifying, and the local Eyewitness News.

No, that's wrong. The censorship is our actual condition; it's this dazzled, exhausted life we lead. We have 78 things to do today, and if we have any real choice left, it's which of these eight kinds of milk will we buy? The censor of the Earth's message is Consumerism, which invented this new kind of taboo: our life is none of our business, while busyness is our life.

The corporations know they must keep the Earth away from us, mediate between this primal force and you and I. Yes, the Earth is an unreliable comrade, roaming around darkly out there beyond the economy of buying and selling.

What's miraculous is that even in this controlled mental environment of consumerism and its virulent subset, militarism, some individuals still sense the Earth behind the wall. We can still hear a message in the sound of the wind in the leaves. If we are in the right mood, a "babbling brook" can be downright articulate.

The belief that the Earth speaks is the strong force at the center of the universe of this book. Every sentence assumes it. In the Church of Stop Shopping we believe that the Earth is the source of new language and meaning. New stories are coming to us in this wind, fire and flood. Our radical performance community — the Stop Shopping Choir — translates the bad weather into song lyrics, singing out from rooftops and fire escapes, in bank lobbies and museums, in front of big box stores and at mountaintop removal sites. Our job is to sing and preach the inspiring message delivered by the latest disaster.

What is that message? Is the Earth daring us with its impossible upheavals to re-enter the scary story of evolution? How do we take the actions we need to take to save ourselves in the natural world, which is poised to overpower the world of greed that raised us? We ask the force of life on Earth — and this is our only defense — can you make us as radical as you are?

As we live through this Sixth Extinction, as wetlands and mountains and species go silent, as we face down our *own* extinction, each of us must discover what we can uniquely do. In this book, I'm putting myself in the role of ghost-writer, asking the Earth to be the author. I turn to the people who have always conversed with the Earth, and it's those whom we have enslaved and slaughtered. I look for a way to write all this: from the borders of expressive trespassing, science fiction, singing activism, non-god Bible-like stories with the Earth replacing the patriarch, prayers to the living and the dead. My aim is to soul-shake us into conjuring a new story for ourselves. We need new kinds of activism, and fast. My fervent hope is that shocking actions will be inspired by these pages.

It comes down to putting our bodies on the line. Time and again, people have done this in order to claim new freedoms: Rosa Parks walks to the empty seat; Cesar Chavez fasts while the grape-pickers hold up cardboard signs on the traffic islands of California; the Stonewall faeries hurl their stilettoes at their police tormentors; the Berrigan brothers pour blood on military draft cards; Wangari Maathi stands by her trees in Nairobi, shaming the strongman hiding behind his guns.

What have we done so far to blaze such change? Considering the apocalyptic scale of the crimes against the Earth, our response so far has been hesitating, predictable and middle-of-the road. We need a new wave of citizen warriors, many thousands of Earth-lovers responding physically. The Earth is calling for — shall we say it? — a Revolution. Revolutions are made of the commitment of the body to the celebration of life, and the risk of its loss is part of the festivities.

We will have to let the Earth put the movement in our movement. All of us will have to do everything we've never done before. We're leaping and floating above the forest floor, through the coral reef, beneath the night stars and into other people's lives. We *are* the extreme weather. We do to ourselves what the storms do to our cities: break down the walls, make the old categories and compartments float like debris that can evolve into new life.

We hear the Earth's voice! The language of the Earth is inside of us, made clear by our all-out risk. The cyclone's 200-mph wind whispers a sweet nothing in our ear: *Commit to Action*.

We'll do what you say.

IT'S A LIFE

WE DRESS UP LIKE EXTINCT ANIMALS and sing in a bank and get arrested and go to jail and try to sleep and then we come home and sleep and get up and dress like extinct animals and get on the subway to another bank where we meet the Stop Shopping singers and go into the lobby and sing and hand out the investment information and then get hand-cuffed and go to jail or maybe just the precinct house for a few hours but maybe the Tombs up to three days and nights and face the judge again and make some promise or other and go home and get ready to go banking. We shower and then study bank investments and then call other shopping stop-pers and — can you believe UBS is bankrolling that Aussie coal? — and more extinction reports and then we dress up like another threatened kind of life and go sing in bank lob-bies and parking lots and drive-through teller windows and bank-sponsored art events and preach inside the circle of faces which are loathing us or giggling or stunned with thought and we hand out information on Earth crimes sponsored by their money and if we stay too long they hand-cuff us and we go to jail or maybe just get a warning in which case we do more research after returning home and love the loved ones and eat and drink and read and wash and do laundry and put off the bills and we're exhausted so we fall asleep and dream of rainforests and prairies and coral reefs and wake up and dress like extinct animals and get on the subway and meet the other singers who are wearing giant pâpier maché heads of the Golden Toad, another casualty of climage change, and off we go to the bank, broke but laughing all the way to the bank, to sing.

SHOPOCALYPSE

Will we survive the fire?
The Shopocalypse, the Shopocalypse
Will we feel the Hell in this shopping list?
The neighbors fade into the shopping mall
The oceans rise but I — I must buy it all!

Shopocalypse!
It ain't the blues
It's convenience

Will we drive fast all night
To the wilderness, to the wilderness?
Will we die of fright when the logos hiss?
Can we go home, break in our own front door?
The TV stops to hear our insides roar!

Shopocalypse!
The problem ain't that we got the blues
It's that damn convenience

THE GOLDEN TOAD
GOES BANKING

WE HAD ARRANGED TO MEET UP at the Manhattan Gourmet Restaurant, a glorified deli at 57th and 6th, right above the F Train station, with the Chase bank looming across the avenue. We carried our toad heads in a big sack.

It was a working-class place with a lunch crowd shouting their orders, lots of laughter. The folks were service workers, spiffily dressed people in retail, Verizon repairmen, security and cleaning people. There were about fifteen of us on this improbable mission: Laura the Diva, Dragonfly, Bryce, Ashlie, Erik Rivas taking pictures, Sylver of Picture the Homeless, Lizzie, Donald Gallagher the Radical Faerie, David Yap and Pat Hornak and Dawn Lookkin and Chido Tsemunhu and Susanna Pryce, and Nehemiah Luckett, our music director.

Looking back at the pictures of our preparations, I see a UPS driver staring at us over his tray of food. We're ages 20 to 75, several skin colors and hairstyles, from Mohawk cornrowed, rainbow-dyed do's to various fades and chops. We're telling each other to breathe, feeling a little giddy and edgy.

We start fitting on our toad heads. Each singer knows which one of the orange cardboard-and-papier-maché constructions fits onto his or her own head. Some of us wear baseball caps to stabilize what amounts to a big off-kilter hat

— the protruding lips of the frog jut out over the forehead, so the beak of the cap helps to keep it up off our eyes.

We had re-conned the bank earlier, and now we're reviewing the route, describing the bank's floor-plan and where the personnel are stationed, where we should walk and who to face when we sing, how to signal to each other that it's time to stop and leave.

The people at the next table, hair salon or nail shop ladies who have been cackling with gossip since we got here, they tell us if we're robbing the bank they want a cut to keep quiet. We tell them, "No, you should pay us, 'cuz we're performing for the workers up there because they get so bored." And a lady with beehive hair like the Shangi-Las from the '60s, she says, "Oh, I know. And those tellers don't get paid anything, minimum, it's terrible. Some of 'em's on welfare. Can you believe that? Working in a bank and getting food stamps?"

We walk out onto the Avenue, a stream of toad-humans. It's raining lightly on our garish, gold-orange reptile heads with the fat black eyeballs. We tread carefully over the potholes in the pavement, steadying our head gear. Following our plan, we stop in the bank's glassy downstairs lobby where there's no security, and in fact, no customers either. A semi-circle of ATM machines — with the blown-up photos of smiling actors with checkbooks — stand there looking lonely in the floor-to-ceiling glass enclave with 6th Avenue streaming by.

The part of the bank that contains our audience is upstairs at the end of a long shiny escalator. At the top is where we want to hop! We chose this bank because of its strange design — this escalator will deposit our radical toads directly into the midst of "wealth management." Whereas most bank designs have a more fortress-like defense of their rich clients from the street, this building leaves them more vulnerable to, shall we say, the natural world.

We circle up, hold hands and pray to the life of the Earth, and to the memory of our animal guide the Golden Toad, and to the thousands of animals that have run, flown, slithered and jumped into extinction. We ask for assistance in our fight with this Devil. Life around the world is under attack by this fossil fuel bank, the old Rockefeller Standard Oil bank that has always paid for the drilling, gouging, scraping, burning and shipping of the flammable blood of the Earth. Chase Bank is currently the top financier of CO_2 emissions. According to Banktrack.org in the Netherlands, it is the single most climate-changing institution on the planet. Sometimes we have so much fun in our church that I have to put the fear of the Devil back into our singers (and myself). Yeah, Chase really IS the Devil.

The toads hop onto the escalator and the action is on. The Stop Shoppers adopt their crouch, elbows flared out, knees bent in our human approximation of long-legged frogs or toads, rising smoothly toward our interruption.

The escalator delivers us to a little landing pad that opens onto a row of teller windows to the left, and I remember the nasal voice of the beehive-hair lady with her tellers-on-welfare story. To the right is a carpeted area where the uptown rich are received. A series of desks and lovely hardwood chairs and little plush couches are a habitat for the six or eight 1%-ers seated with their portfolio managers. The priests of money sit at their computers, reviewing the returns for their demure clients. The rich are here in the middle of the day —

elegant women, who upon seeing us become suddenly frozen into impassive-faced John Singer Sargent poses, their eyes lidded, chins turned away, not wanting to admit that a choir of singing extinct reptiles and an Elvis impersonator preacher type seem to have taken over the bank.

Nehemiah has the singers blazing:

I'm a frog, I'm a tiger, I'm a manta ray
I'm a life in the great death wave.
Extinction is my name,
Call me Climate Change!

Everything happens at once. Some of the bankers leave the room, some converge on us, and some sit with the rich ladies as if consoling them. I'm preaching, "Stop this banking! Hear the demands of the spirits of life you have killed!" Nehemiah is comforting people, "This is a protest about your investments. It will be over in a minute." Lizzie is handing out our research. The toads are moving through the maze of desks, hopping, jerking their black-eyed masks back and forth, fingers splayed out the way frogs do, and always singing the song.

The song's point of view is an expression from threatened life: *I'm a bat, I'm an aspen, I'm a wolverine / I'm a banker's wildest dream.* As the preacher, I'm shouting into the gaps of the song the way I've learned to do in our concert shows. "This is life singing! —— Living things giving you —— your profit report —— your drills, your explosives —— your poisons!"

Five minutes, then ten minutes go by. Laura and Dragonfly are walking between the desks, boldly crossing away from the area in front of the teller windows where I'm preaching. Laura's grandfather was a leader at the World Bank. She's not afraid of the rich and their bankers. Dragonfly is fearless too, but from another angle. Her dad was a lifer in the army. Back when Standard Oil was founded her family was just coming out of slavery.

The boldest soldiers from the other side also come to joust. There is one classic red-in-the-face type with the old saw about private property and the police are on their way and YOU MUST LEAVE THIS ESTABLISHMENT! THIS IS A CRIME! The toads surround him. Toad-power is real. Consider the species that adopted us with its history: the Golden Toads were killed off in two years by a blast-furnace-hot El Niño that dried up their mountain ponds — this, after having evolved as a species for a million years.

It's good activism to remember the heart of your purpose at the point when you are most challenged, and that banker backed down in the face of a pile-up of angry life. The lyrics of the song anticipate opposition: *We surround you / You take the names of what you kill / We may be dead but we still sing / We surround you.* And so the red-faced warrior was surrounded by vengeful toad ghosts. Rough.

Now the extraordinary interruption of the ritual quiet of the bank is creating eddies and swirls of activity across the desks and partitions. Different reactions set in. Bankers are giggling, shouting into phones, frozen and silent, staring out the window. One loan officer is smiling and laughing, taking a movie with his cell phone, like it's for his kids. Meanwhile, the Golden Toads are singing at the top of their lungs. *We surround you! / We surround you! / We may be dead but we still sing!*

As adrenalized as I was with my preaching, I remember loving what was happening, thinking, *this* is church. The life on Earth that we have given ourselves up to, surrendered to, is coming to life here! The dead are singing! It's *Resurrection Time!*

There is the impending arrival of the police to be concerned about, but we must also avoid the increasing risk of our own anger. Although we're trained in nonviolence, we can become worried that we're not breaking through, and then naturally we want to apply more force. We feel we must sing and preach louder because of this banker-blowhard in the foreground, but also because of our own fear that we aren't doing enough.

I want to stay and have debriefings with each banker and each wealthy customer: "Do you get it? Will you ask yourselves some questions about Chase? Is divestment a possibility? Are we getting through? After all, given the Earth's crisis, this sober and elite separation from the reality of your investments must end. This bank must be interrupted by all citizens, all the time — *to save our lives.*"

I feel myself being pulled from my perch on a window seat. It's time to go. I go on a bit more, "STOP BANKING, START LIVING! THIS EXTINCTION WAVE IS RISING WITH YOUR PROFIT! WHAT KIND OF ECONOMY DEPENDS ON MASS DEATH?"

Now Nehemiah has got me by the polyester lapels, "It's time. It's been fifteen minutes. Let's get out of here." The toads are also having difficulty stopping their hopping. Several of our troupe are highly trained underemployed method actors. Their hopping is so convincing you'd think their legs are fifteen feet long. But Nehemiah is able to wade out into the pond we have created here and collar the toads. They finally do stop their hopping, take off their toad heads, and walk toward the silver moving stairs to descend.

We re-cross the Avenue. It isn't raining anymore. So much has happened that it feels surprising that the Manhattan Gourmet Restaurant is the same as it was when we left it, but that was only twenty minutes ago. They had kindly allowed us to leave our backpacks behind the counter, and now they let us reach over and grab our stuff. We say goodbye, and maybe we spend a little too much time with the hugs and thanks.

We go down into the subway, at perhaps too leisurely a pace. And the singers do manage to commute to freedom. Nehemiah and I, however, are caught by the police on the station's platform still holding our damning evidence, the sack of toad heads. We have six officers surrounding us. We're cuffed in front of our fellow commuters and led away.

Escorted back up to the street, the police decide to leave us in the glass ATM lobby. The lunch hour crowd gawks at the black man and the sad preacher in handcuffs surrounded by now an incredible number of cops. Forty? Fifty? *All these cops!* — lots of New York's Finest, standing there studying us.

Who knows how long we were there — a half hour? More? I know that more people witnessed us standing there than come to a year's worth of our shows at the Public Theater. We gathered around us a sizeable group of mildly scandalized citizens, and a flotilla of police, cruisers with lights pumping. Nehemiah was amazing, laughing the whole time. He acted like it was a reality show.

One John Wayne-like cop, older and clearly in charge,

came down on Nehemiah for his good humor. "You think this is funny?" "Well, yes it is," I replied. "We are extinct animals in a protest." Nehemiah added, "Extinct animals who don't appreciate being extinct . . . " The white shirt looked at us like he'd bitten into a piece of bad meat. Then he jerked back to attention. "Okay, whatever your weird religion is, we're taking you in."

Finally, we were told to get our asses into the back seat of a cruiser, our handcuffs making us lie sideways. The precinct house for crimes committed in the Broadway and Times Square area is called "Midtown North." At 54th St and 8th Avenue, it wasn't far away, but mid-town is a constant traffic jam so it took a while. John Wayne was already waiting for us when we got there, with his pen and forms laid out on the desk, ready to process us into jail. Bummer.

It could have been a more severe bummer. The police in the front seat, wending their way through the midtown traffic while we were pretzeled in the backseat, told us that a hysterical woman in the bank had locked herself in a bathroom and called 911, sobbing and retching and proclaiming that she wouldn't unlock the bathroom door until the police arrived. "I need to save myself from bank robbers in animal masks . . . " She incited a robbery-in-progress alert, a Code 19 went out, and police were running red lights all over Manhattan to get to our toad pond.

So, no, we didn't think that was funny. That was not good. Somebody could have gotten hurt. We had thought we were being clear enough with our explanations and the comic appearance of the toad masks. We had thought that the singing, though certainly forceful, was also entertaining.

Nehemiah and I sat in the cell a while together, the sad cage rich with the smells of Times Square drunks and pickpockets. We let out a long exhale, weighing the day's blur of events.

Our softly spoken conversation had the oxygen burned out of it by the stare of Captain Wayne. And, we murmured to each other, we are . . . we are *so* in the system. John Wayne will put us so deep in Kafka world, that is to say, so deeply incarcerated in the city jail (known to locals as "the Tombs"), it ain't funny. "Looks like we're going downtown," I said. "The issue is not in doubt," answered Nehemiah, maestro of the singing toads.

Suddenly Officer Beaudette, an old friend from our dozens of arrests downtown at Union Square, bursts into the police station. Beaudette plants himself between the sad prisoners and the triumphing moralist of stage and screen. "Hi Jack," says Officer Beaudette. (Oh, maybe his name *is* John Wayne.) Then Officer Beaudette sees us. "Billy! Another protest! That was you at the bank??!! How's your daughter, she must be four now, right?"

Oh! Oh my god. Beaudette is the Captain of Midtown North! He's been stationed up here! When Captain Beaudette indicated that he knew my family, that turned John Wayne into Robin Williams in *Patch Adams*. Well, maybe not that cuddly. But he stopped sending us to the Tombs at that moment. Resurrection Time! Officer Beaudette, a man who put me in the Tombs probably twenty times when he worked at the Union Square precinct, said, "Oh sign the Rev and his friend out. They're good for their word. Get Rev back to Lena." And turning to me, "Got a picture?"

We had thought the toads would be like Disney characters, poignant and political for the people who did get it, and outlandish and comic for the people who didn't. For those who did, well, those people would remember the natural world and connect their work in the bank to its consequences. But that lady in the bathroom unleashing the NYPD? She freaked out. That shouldn't happen.

And a couple of months later, in court, the District Attorney's office imitated the upset woman. They called our action a "menace" and a "riot," and urged the judges (a series of four of them over the next six months) to send Nehemiah to jail for three months, and said that I should go in for a full year.

Eventually, the Assistant DA, a young crypto-yuppie type who had long ago abandoned himself to assholishness, told the last in the assembly line of Manhattan municipal judges, "Your honor, on further review we have determined that these are entertainment professionals and this was a musical presentation."

Nehemiah walked. I was consigned to an afternoon of "community service," cleaning the benches and viewing area of the Statue of Liberty. I selfied myself with brooms and black rubber gloves and much love poured in on Twitter . . .

Postscript: We asked press professionals to estimate the number of "media exposures" posted about this story of a musical, Earth-political action that had been staged inside a wealth-management Chase Bank branch. The estimates were between 80 and 100 million exposures, and in a good number of these, the causal connection of Chase's investments and climate change was stated in the first sentences of text. This was the case with NPR, and *The Guardian*, the *Village Voice* and *Grist*, *Forbes* and the Huffington Post.

Do we know if this media attention to the information offered up by a comic-political-spiritual (that is to say, very weird because un-categorizable) troupe in New York resulted in a significant number of customers pulling their money out of JPMorgan Chase? We have no way of knowing that.

But we don't expect measurable impacts from our work, not in this case. The point is, most of us usually don't think of banks as financing climate change. The process of education about this has barely begun. To change a critical mass of citizens on this issue, it will take far more evidence than we can present in one action, one trial, some press, and a run at the Public Theater.

On the other hand, we successfully presented a civics lesson: this isn't a question only of information, policy, litigation and lobbying   the solution must be *spiritual*. What we need is an escape from our habitual human-centered fundamentalism.

In the Church of Stop Shopping, we know that behind whatever campaign it is that we're working on, the Earth whispers to us like the ultimate conscience: There must be a change in how we imagine, express, sense life, and how we love.

WHAT IS THE NAME
OF THIS STORM?

WE LIVE NEAR THE ATLANTIC OCEAN, in Brooklyn, New York. I'm writing in early February 2013, about three months after Hurricane Sandy. Now another big storm is spinning out of the sea and everybody's jumpy.

I shoveled snow for an hour this afternoon, feeling the wind begin with a slow growling. Then I climbed the steps to our apartment, where Savitri and almost three years old Lena have come back early from the city. Savi is checking food provisions and flashlights — but is tonight's storm so deadly? We bring up satellite pictures of the thing. It looks like a hurricane all right, like a white circular saw the size of New England, its serrated edge cutting the coast. It has that eye in the center.

There is a difference with this new winter storm. The National Weather Service was surprised to find that it had lost its naming rights by some mysterious sleight of hand — to the Weather Channel, with its ads, graphics, and "on-camera meteorologists." The Weather Channel's anchor, a toothy blonde, smiles at us from the computer screen with the satellite shot over her shoulder, as if she's taking a selfie with a 10,000-Hiroshimas storm system. And why should she give the storm any particular regard? Her bosses have named it "Nemo," after the cute orange clownfish star of the 3-D blockbuster from Pixar, the animation studio founded by Steve Jobs and marketed by Mickey Mouse.

After *Finding Nemo* grossed almost a billion dollars worldwide, most families with children were left with a vivid memory of dazzling coral reefs, shark chases, pratfalls, and kidnappings by goofy scuba divers. Finally, the adorable Nemo, with his identity problems, developmentally disabled fin and voice of Albert Brooks, wins the heart of fellow clownfish "Dory," voice by Ellen DeGeneres.

As night falls in Brooklyn, the howls of wind are joined by muffled winter thundering. This will be an ominous "thundersnow" blizzard, with hail and dunes of snow. Reports are coming in from Massachusetts. Houses and cars and people are lost in the white-out. I go down and shovel once more by the light of the street lamp, but then give up. I peer into the flurries, thinking, "You are now a billion-dollar clownfish. Were you aware of that?"

There is something in the grand violence of the wind, I can almost hear the storm answer me: "NEMO? Not hardly." Then I go over into what I call *climate change mind*. Hmmm . . . there is something fishy about this storm. That strange sighing thunder is the underwater vacuum of vanished fisheries, the thousand-mile dead zones shooting the last schools of blue-fin tuna and cod and haddock and sea trout and striped bass up into the accelerating darkness. Ghosts of flying fish are whipping through the bare maple trees on our Brooklyn street. The streetlights are flickering.

The life of the ocean is carried in this stinging snow, battling the billion-dollar vaudeville fish for our hearts and minds. I see the neighborhood children's heads peeking out of the glowing windows, drawn by the power and mystery of the natural world bearing down upon us, but I know their heads are full of Nemo, too. The fish are dying and the memories of fish are being commodified.

I am one of those people who believe that these storms are much deadlier because of us. But I suspect that I am another progressive type who is still, at heart, a climate skeptic. I must be. What have I done for this storm? What do I owe this wind? It has gaseous acids in it. The bleached coral of the Caribbean is drumming on our house. But I keep my guilt nice and abstract. It is so easy to believe the climate science but then go about our digitized day with the extreme weather and consumer culture in a desperate fight to the death, as if all that takes place in a separate world.

There is nothing separate about it. That world is our bodies. This song-and-dance fish is swimming in our eyes and ears. It is telling focus group–tested jokes on screens in the palms of our hands. And I'm getting spooked by the ghoulish soundtrack. The wind is like a thousand swordfish flying out of the cracking branches. There is living death inside this storm. The wind is way over the speed limit on the Brooklyn Queens Expressway. It's blowing my lips to the Manhattan side of my face. I'd better go inside.

Finally, later that night I ask the question — who owns the Weather Channel, anyway? Answer: Comcast, the largest media conglomerate in the world, owner of cable companies, NBC, Telemundo, Time Warner, theme parks, and much of the high-speed internet trade. It is among the top lobbyists in Washington and the avowed foe of Net neutrality.

Another Weather Channel investor is Bain Capital, of Mitt Romney fame.

What is going on here? The 40 million people in the storm's path have had Nemo or National Geographic shark porn or that macho Australian guy who got killed by a stingray pasted over their memory of what an ocean is. In our minds and on our screens we sustain the luminescence of Nemo's reef as the actual storm roars around us, coming in off the dark ocean.

And what would we see if this actual ocean's life *was our media*, as it was for millennia in the souls of our ancestors? Can we ever get back to the thrilling drama of the ocean? If we were capable of outmaneuvering Pixar and Disney, Comcast and NBC, and in doing so escape to that beautiful storm of sea-life, would we find that the evolution of 500 million years, a watery cathedral of interdependency, is a now a vast crime scene? It would be an elemental shock for us. Would we know how to care for the poisoned seed of this big storm? We would have to begin to evolve a new kind of human being. Then we might get the name right.

Lena thinks she hears voices in the grumbling thunder. I hear her ask, "What is the storm saying, Dad?" I have to take a moment. I want the answer for myself, too. "Well, the storm comes out of the ocean, from the other side of Coney Island. We're supposed to remember its name, because it is very old and it came a long way to get here. But we forgot it because we were busy, full of business, and now the storm is shouting its name through the city and all the towns. Let's listen."

A PRAYER
TO THE DEAD

ARE YOU LISTENING? MAYBE NOT. You'll tell me somehow.

Instruct us. No zombies from the *Game of Thrones*, please, we need the real dead.

You were just here, weren't you? Taking your own turn being alive. And now you are beyond life, in that place before we're born and after we die. When I walk in a forest the leaves flicker with the births and deaths. Some of these insects live a couple of days. My gratitude isn't that sophisticated yet, I mean really, to give thanks to an insect? But will you teach me?

Our little nonprofit theater company needs some props for our next play, which is about a church with an unknowable god. Would you donate please, bless us with portable eco-systems that we can carry into the Earth-killing bank lobbies? May we leave ponds and forests and Dakota plains and Appalachian mountaintops there on the shiny tiles. May life bloom, as perplexed bankers get the return of life on their bad investments!

Oh death on Earth, we pray for the privilege of our resurrection, straight from the stinky, sticky stardust, right into our new job as super weeds, super pests. It would be an honor to be wild.

May we be unafraid of the death that life has waiting inside of it. Let me imagine my last instant fondly: "Oh! Here it is. I'm dying." Is this the real birth of change?

Bless my daughter with a loving memory of me. May she recall an Elvis impersonator reading her thousands of books on the F-train. Yes, I would love to be the good dead.

And while I'm alive, give me the power to not disappoint the whole collective of the dead. All of you. All the living that entered the state of death, you make a superior intelligence. You are deciding what to do with the remaining humans on Earth, we who are ending the life around us.

We are so blessed by the compassionate leadership of you dead. It has converted our fear of joining you into the happiness of direct action against those who create extinction. The dead are with us in force.

Oh the Lifealujah of a good action!

Amen.

GOOD OR BAD
VS. LIVE OR DIE

IN THE WORLD OF ENVIRONMENTAL ADVOCACY, there are two kinds of orgs. There are the big outfits like the Sierra Club who try to make us more good, and less bad. All the big money NGOs, with the profound exception of Greenpeace, are in the "Good or Bad" category.

Then there are the "Live or Die" people. These groups have names like Center for Biological Diversity and Mountainkeepers and Global Justice Now. They don't ask the question "Do you want to be good?" They ask, "Do you want to live?" Their read on the data coming in from natural scientists is that we have a decision to make about our survival. This is completely different than being "good" — the bromides of ethical shopping and carbon trading are to these folks an infuriating distraction. They say: Confront death and do what it takes to live.

The "Live or Die" people know that action must be taken immediately. And so they take on the aggressive narcotics of consumer culture, the advertising, the debt, the daily exhaustion, the sports and porn and celebrities.

The impact of living-through-products is a dazzling gradualism, for individuals and for institutions as well. How is it possible to penetrate the mental environment of consumer society and shout, "There Is A Terrible Emergency Here!" How can we *act,* when heroism, genius, courage, heightened emotionality, and all the desperate cliffhanger plots are already being used to sell us products?

"Good or Bad" is just where consumerism wants us, back in the predictable stories that tell us, "You can be sure of yourself, with lots of planning, projections, number crunching."

"Live or Die" explodes with creativity and necessary confusion. We forgive ourselves in advance for that confusion, amen? We know sometimes mayhem is what creates the next thing. We are saving ourselves, and it's got to be at least partly, well, a miracle. Something we don't understand. Like love!

While the corporations are trying to halt our advance by selling us a product called "Saving Ourselves," we will have already evolved, because that's where "Live or Die" gets you. "Live or Die" is what the furry, scaled and feathered citizens of a wild ecosystem do. They save their lives while life saves them.

EXILES ON
MAIN STREET

IT SEEMS LIKE EVERY WEEK OR SO you can hear language borrowed from the War on Terror, the Salem Witch Hunts and the House Un-American Activities Committee hearings. Some prosecutor somewhere will be hurling invective at fossil fuel resisters, who sit in the courtroom with their pro bono lawyers, staring with the disbelief of newcomers to Evil.

We know of the heroes like the Sea Shepherd sailors, the Arctic 30, and Tim "Bidder 70" DeChristopher. And though some of these activists are young, we tend to think of them as veterans who are making a stand for the rest of us. But a new movement is building, in which the heroes are people who might be described as amateurs. These are "regular citizens" making a stand against fossil fuel projects where they live, people who are resisting with their bodies, with no organization behind them, no money, no backing. And something about these under-equipped protesters is making Big Oil go crazy.

Three Michigan women — Lisa Leggio, Barbara Carter, and Vicki Hamlin — chained themselves to an excavator in the little town of Mason. They were polite in that Midwestern way throughout their protest of Enbridge, the Canadian firm that leaked 800,000 gallons of oil in their community and can't seem to clean it up. After their guilty verdict was pronounced, Judge William Collette, a Republican and former bomber pilot marched the ladies — one of them a great-grandmother — straight to jail from their defense table, despite their intentions to appeal.

Here we have a signature tactic of fossil fuel justice. Call it "overcharging," accusing nonviolent defendants of felonious crimes that will later be dropped, but meanwhile holding them in prison because the bail is set high, to match the seriousness of the specious charges. In this way, the personal turmoil for the accused and their family is maximized, and worse, this is how the State and its partner corporations cast a pall of guilt on the innocent, making them look dark and dangerous on the local evening news. This is an effect that lingers on in their community, with obvious long lasting side effects.

Over-charging can also quickly slide into creative charges that rewrite the law. Our American alphabet soup of domestic security agencies — the DHS, NSA and FBI — is trying out a new charge on some banner-droppers in Oklahoma City. Two activists in the Great Plains Tar Sands Resistance are facing charges on perpetrating a "Bioterrorism Hoax" at the headquarters of extraction giant Devon Energy. Now it seems that protesters could become liable for exciting the morbid imaginations of police. When some cheap glitter shook out from one of the banners, the police reasoned that this might be chemical warfare. Stefan Warner and Moriah Stephenson are facing ten years in prison.

Overkill is easy when you're Enbridge and Devon Energy, companies whose assets are in the $30 to $45 billion range. And behind the front line of the fossil fuel companies are the banks that finance them, such as Bank of America and Chase, HSBC and Royal Bank of Scotland. The fossil-fuel-investing banks are bigger than most countries, with assets measured in the trillions. And when these giants look over the shoulders of the prosecutors and see someone whom everyone seems to know, someone who lives over on Elm Street standing up to them, what do they see? Was anything further outside of their business plan?

Yet, even with the corrupting influence of Big Oil, the efforts to cast these homemade activists as dark assassins often backfires.

Vera Scroggins lives in a heavily hydrofractured area near the town of Montrose, in northeastern Pennsylvania. She has non-violently but flamboyantly opposed the oil companies, even organizing a rally with Yoko Ono and Sean Lennon. The Cabot Oil and Gas Company now owns much of the property rights in and around Montrose, with a tangle of difficult-to-understand leases and easements, as well as mineral rights beneath the homes of long-time citizens. Cabot is so upset with Ms. Scroggins, a 63-year-old grandmother, that they persuaded a judge to issue an injunction that forbids her from walking anywhere on the 312 square miles around Montrose that Cabot somehow controls, including the town's surface above minerals controlled by the company far below. This puts her under virtual house arrest. After being tailed by police for a few days, she realized that she couldn't figure out where it was legal for her to go. She couldn't walk to the pharmacy or her favorite diner. Scroggins has, surreally, asked the court for a map with legal trails through her own hometown.

The more innocent the protester, the more terrified the billionaire's men. Grandmother Scroggins showed up in court to face the wall of suits, the six Cabot lawyers. So they made her the exile on Main Street. But do they really believe that will be enough? Doesn't Vera Scroggins resemble the citizen volunteers who showed up early in the civil rights movement, the peace and gender rights movements? Isn't this entrenched power's historical nightmare, returning again to haunt them? The willingness to risk personal injury, jail time, or worse have made these "ordinary people" into legendary figures. And these folks have kids and grandkids. What if more citizens really listen to what the scientists are saying and realize they have nothing to lose but their loved ones — won't this make them the fiercest warriors of all?

You can't stop Vera Scroggins, or the Enbridge Three, or the Oklahoma City glitterati. You can't stop the families who over-ran the fracking equipment in West Sussex. You can't stop Bo Webb, the ex-marine in the coal-blasted mountains of West Virginia. You can't stop Idle No More, the natives in Canada and Utah blocking tar sands equipment from their sacred lands. You can't stop the young UK activists who climbed EDF Energy's smokestack and stopped those emissions for a week. You can't stop Grace Cagle from living in a pipeline-blocking treehouse in Texas. You can't stop the Zapatistas, the ultimate revolution by nonprofessionals in the mountains of Chiapas, still going strong after more than twenty years. You can't stop Drew Hutton and the Lock the Gate ranchers in Queensland and New South Wales. You can't stop the Grandmothers Knitting Against Gas; or Wahleah Johns and the Navajo community trying to go solar; or Yvon Raoul in Alberta, playing bagpipes against tar sands; or the Liberate Tate museum-invaders, trying to strip big oil of the prestige of fine arts.

There are too many Vera Scroggins to chase down, and too many to publicly defame, and too many to lock up. The irresistible force of the changing Earth and the supposedly immoveable object of the fossil fuel industry are going to have a fight to the death. Whatever sort of apocalypse we're in for, the Earth will survive. And in the end, I bet, Vera will walk wherever she wants to.

RIVER SONG

You want to take our river
Tunnel deep under the Hudson
Take our river
Leaking gas in the schoolyard

You want to take our river
Engines dig with their teeth
In the deep dark water
Things we cannot see

You can't
You can't
You can't take my home
You can't take my place
You, You, You, You
You can't take my bed
You can't take my fire
Can't can't can't
Can't force my love
You can't take my life

You want to take our river
Flowing by in silence
You want to take our neighbor
Burn us with your greed

You want to take our river
Where it meets the sea
But a wave will stop you
Things you cannot see

ANNIE
MARIE

We need the things we cannot see
We see the things we cannot be
We know the things we can't understand
We stand in wonder not knowing the plan

THE HUDSON
COMES ASHORE

AFTER THE UNFORGETTABLE EIGHT WEEKS of our Zuccotti Park residence, as the Occupy Wall Street movement evolved into 80 working groups operating out of apartments and church basements, among the strongest was the "Environmental Solidarity Working Group." We were amazed on our first visit to see Occupy veterans sitting next to uptown people from the Sierra Club next to Hispanic grandmothers from community gardens.

By the spring of 2012, the immediate Devil that we all agreed on was the Spectra Pipeline, a fracked gas tube of poison coming into Manhattan from the drilling sites in Pennsylvania. The pipeline pierced through a series of communities — all of whom had voted against the pipeline's passage by schools and highways and residences — but no one could stop its advance. Democracy could not oppose a pipeline backed by Wall Street and Big Oil. They just rolled over all the votes and the pipeline kept coming. This was a remarkable show of fossil fuel chutzpah, and this was our Devil.

The pipeline was scheduled to tunnel under the Hudson River and surface at the Gansevoort Street pier in the old Meatpacking District in the West Village, across the West Side Highway from the new downtown Whitney Museum. We saw an opportunity to perform there, making the site of the pipeline our stage. Here was the natural beauty of the grand Hudson River, deep and wide and formidable as it nears the ocean, with Lady Liberty visible just to the south. Our guess was that less than 5% of New Yorkers had any idea that this high-pressure flammable concoction was about to shoot into their midst.

The Gansevoort pier was covered with city garbage trucks, huge vehicles resembling hulking, ancient beasts. The ground being worked by the drills and bulldozers getting ready to secure the pipeline was on the north edge of the pier, near the waves and old rotting wood from long ago piers. Fifty yards south was the playground pier, which had been re-created for the children in the shape of an old sailing ship; the "deck" of the pier jutted out into the Hudson, with flags and ropes in the air. The children would be playing in the blast-zone of this gas.

Our first foray would be a ritual here, to confuse the serpent as it surfaced to hook up with the Con Ed grid. We did in fact begin to think of the pipeline as a serpent, and it seemed like one, as reports came in from Jersey City and all the towns along its route. It was burrowing through just under the surface of the ground, with highways and schools in its blast-zone, on the move toward the Apple.

We snuck onto the site, wearing gauzy hazmat-like suits, looking like a cross between beekeepers and astronauts. We carried rolls of pink polka dots, and we rolled out the adhesive-backed vinyl-like material on the ground between the excavators' machinery, pulled off the big dots and began to cover the bulldozers and trucks with the cartoonish spots.

And the hazmatted liberators, having encountered no

security personnel at all (this first time), left the construction site shot through with a comic visual effect. The polka-dotted digging site was in full view of the West Side Highway and a potential object of hilarity, or so it seemed to us as we peeled off our costumes and fled to a local watering hole.

We left kindly messages for the workers — we knew we were impugning the macho world of earth-moving and construction. Some of the garbage truck drivers we talked to during our operation found our explanations made good sense. And these city workers didn't like idea of the fracked gas coming through their work site anyway.

We released photos of our antics to the press, which mostly ignored us.

One of our favorite theaters to perform in is the Highline Ballroom, a short four blocks from the Gansevoort serpent-surfacing site. Our show there on one very hot summer afternoon took its theme and its audience outside. The songs and sermons that day were about the love of the river and respect for its power:

> *You want to take our river*
> *Where it meets the sea*
> *But a wave will stop you*
> *Things you cannot see*

> *We need the things we cannot see*
> *We see the things we cannot be*
> *We know the things we can't understand*
> *We stand in wonder not knowing the plan*

We awarded "Fabulous Sainthood" to the brave activists of the SANE Energy Project, who were fighting the Spectra Pipeline and the other four fracked-gas pipelines threatening New York from different sides. We passed the plate and raised $800 for them.

After the Church of Stop Shopping show, our altar call was to walk the faithful out to the playground pier near the digging site. The temperature on this summer day was in the mid-90s, so we brought along water, and members of the choir kept an eye out for dehydration. A couple hundred people walked gamely along the edge of the West Side Highway with us, down to the pier.

People in our group donned the hazmat costumes to emphasize the toxicity of the poisons in the pipeline, and this contrasted weirdly with the children playing on the pier. We handed out information to the bemused and then increasingly concerned parents. A flammable pipeline, right here?

We got out the colored umbrellas that Savitri had prepared, which unfurled side by side to spell out STOP THE PIPELINE. We arranged everyone along the edge of the pier, tilting the umbrellas over the water. One umbrella-person was missing, having wandered off to a bathroom, taking their letter with them. He went for his pee, taking a P from "Pipeline," a key letter in our message. So Savitri took an empty spare umbrella and some toothpaste that a friend had in her purse, and created a toothpaste P.

Soon we were ready for our picture. As the choir sang and I shouted about the Devil Serpent on my bullhorn, photographers from across the way got the long phrase spelled out on the colored umbrellas, as the children continued their play in the background.

Now, this visual received more attention. Our crowd showed the opposition to be large in number, and the playground so close to the pipeline terminus underscored the danger. The image became a viral presence on social forums, recognized by fracking activists in other U.S. cities, in the UK and Ireland, and in Australia, as well. The photos of the pink-spotted heavy equipment were revived, too, as people clicked and dragged and shared the playful action.

But the pleasure that our project was getting attention was dampened when the regulators capitulated to the bank and the oil company. Approval (or rubber-stamping) came in from the Federal Energy Regulatory Commission (FERC), and things started looking bad.

Our escalating narrative now proposed going out onto the river itself for the next direct action. This was Savitri's plan. She had been Queen of the Mermaid Parade at Coney Island four years before and had a deeply involved marine-life activism, shall we say. Whereas previously we had remained high and dry, or perhaps had occasionally been sprayed by waves hitting the rip-rap along the piers, now it was time for some deep water baptism. This next iteration of the pipeline resistance would involve a canoe and three beauties, mermaid-nakedness, death by poisoning, and a bulldozer blade.

The action would be a drama: two women representing the spirit of the river would find a health-conscious jogger who had been overcome by the poisons from the pipeline, dead among the rocks on the shore. The spirit women would carry her body to the machines that claw holes in the river-bank to shoot the gas through, and they would leave it there for an open-casket viewing, there on the yellow blade of the big machine.

The fat little canoe that carried the river women was a homemade one, with a hinge in the middle for folding it in two and carrying it easily in the flatbed of a pickup. The canoe belonged to Lopi, who had made it, and we carried it to the site on top of our 1985 Mercedes station wagon, the faithful old beater. There was a launch for kayakers and ciga-rette boats on wheels five or six city blocks upstream from Gansevoort pier. The two river women, Monica and Lopi, pushed the canoe from the boat launch and out into the river, which caught the boat with its no-nonsense power, turned it and pointed it south, and they went with the flow.

Savi, in her jogging outfit, waited on the rip-rap of Gan-sevoort pier, with the garbage trucks above her. The rest of us watched from the playground pier. Savitri tried to look around the edge of things north along the riverbank, as Lopi paddled her sea-green-and-blue boat with Monica in the bow. They stayed close to the buildings and docks on the Manhat-tan side, not getting out into the dark deep of the river. Sud-denly, there they were, our friends looking like an oil painting of river nymphs, serene in this otherworldly little drama.

Their bodies were painted green and blue, Occupy radi-cals with a mermaid veneer, and decidedly not your Disney-type little mermaid. These two furies are long drinks of water, and we, their audience, appreciated the quality of riverness, of old myth. They had their own authority, moving gravely, slowly.

Monica emerged from the water while Lopi steadied the

boat. Savitri jogged the length of the Gansevoort landfill and then she fell, overcome by poisonous fumes leaking from the pipeline. Monica found her, limp and lying half in the water, and she pulled the dying woman up from the ground, half-carrying her with an arm thrown over her shoulder. They stumbled together over the rock refuse around the dig, and then they fell.

Recovering, Monica lifted Savitri and carried her again. The seriousness of task of the delivery of the dead to the great poisoner was driving the activism here, the force of the drama. Monica and Savitri struggled toward the culprit, climbing across the broken rocks and churned up landfill the rest of the way. The women held to the stately pace of a ritual, sometimes stopping entirely as figures in a frieze. The whole scene sank into the mythic past and seemed to turn to sepia, as if these women had emerged from the river of time and were expressing the sorrow of the Earth.

Monica laid Savitri's body out in the blade of the yellow bulldozer, then made her way back to the boat. The river spirits regarded the woman on the claw for a time, and then blended back into the water with that same thoughtful ancient descent down over the edge of the river.

This was the final dramatic gesture of the action. The sound of the audience's applause, mostly activists and children on the playground pier with their mothers and dads, faded out into the lapping of the waves on the old pilings and rocks, and the honking of New Yorkers on the West Side Highway.

Looking back

Writing this now, two years later, I feel the presence of the deaths of ten people from gas explosions in Harlem and in the East Village. It is probable that the Spectra Pipeline was the source of the gas. Fracked gas is volatile, and there is danger in the old pipelines and valves of New York City. But the more broadly present danger might be what leaks from our stovetops as we cook, the toxic fracked gas with its carcinogens floating in the air, as we breathe in the radioactivity of the radon that has not yet degraded into a safer, inert element.

Savitri might have represented the death of democracy that day, dead on the yellow claw, hovering over the hole in the riverbank drilled and dug without the permission of the citizens in its blast-zone. That is the direct political meaning. But then there was something else we felt that day too, something more basic, the death by poison, and the riverbank recast for killing.

Savi wore the costume of Hudson Park, the recreational running outfit. There is a picture of health at the river's edge, of greenery and fresh air, and the aforementioned playground on the pier–turned–pirate ship. As is so often the case, the advertisement of modern high-rent life with a river view is an image that we walk into, and in inhabiting it, declare that the advertising is real life. Then the toxins claim the jogger, and the river's surviving oracles are alerted.

The action that day was a tragedy, like an opera but slow and ancient in its aspect, more like a passion play, and it left us with the gift of sorrowful emotions that we might not otherwise have admitted to ourselves. Those of us who take it upon ourselves to become angry and then get to work on a direct action campaign, well, we sometimes forget to stop and just feel what is actually happening, feel the sadness of the goings-on in our home.

Savi didn't ask me to consult on her story. I would have urged more confrontation and complication. She was wise to keep her distance. She was coaxing memories to the surface of the river. And I believe that she was intuiting our hurricane, and the drownings in backyards, in cars that stall, in hallways and attics. The super storm would soon raise this river over its banks.

A culture of resistance is made of an ecosystem of stories, receiving and giving back many meanings. Around Savitri's ritual drowning were the memories of pink polka dots plastered on the earth-movers and a crowd of people spelling out STOP THE PIPELINE. More and more actions followed — a phalanx of green people stopped traffic, others climbed the cranes to make banner drops. Lawsuits were filed and Tim DeChristopher visited from Harvard Divinity and spoke to the activists. Nonviolent direct actions went on for a time, with something happening every week. Marches and rallies, colorful dramas at the Gansevoort site continued on for two years. And still the serpent dug beneath the river, coming closer every day.

We didn't stop the gas that time. That serpent has pierced the West Village, and the pipeline is now hooked into the city's grid. The pipelines like Spectra, of which there are at least five that I'm aware of, are arousing citizen resistance. The one success so far has been at the Port Ambrose facility off Long Island. That risky oil tanker docking site was to have made it possible to sail the crude to foreign markets in special refrigerator ships the size of the Empire State Building, and it was stopped by SANE and a local populace that could see the potential disaster in its design.

This is the brutal frontline, the citizen attempts to stop the spread of the fossil fuel infrastructure, and it is happening around the world. In New York, it seems like Big Oil has been given a sort of wartime footing, blessed with blanket permission for its projects since 9/11. Or maybe this was always the case, with the official go-ahead overriding local voters, health officials, families, and most every interested party, including artists and activists like us, who read our script in the river and the sea.

The women emerging from the water that day — I will never forget it. Soaking wet, big-eyed, a walk across the rubble toward a revealing, the whole thing making a still moment. Savitri and Monica and Lopi created a spiritual activism by entering a larger truth, one we often fail to notice. The strongest media, it turns out, is life and death in the flesh.

ON THE SUBWAY
WITH LENA AND DAD

I GET ON THE TRAIN WITH LENA at the Prospect Park Station. We descend the cold clammy stairs and walk through the automatic doors into the train. At five years old, Lena immediately explores the personalities on the benches along the walls of this metal tube that screeches under New York. She knows that if she and her dad can sit side by side, that we can read a book on our trip to school, a 40-minute ride.

Lena also knows that if she can squeeze in between two people and dad can maneuver to stand over her in the strap-hanging crowd, steadying himself with one hand while reading her book upside down, she can still get the story. She knows by now that giving up your seat to a kid and a mom or a dad is standard child-friendly courtesy.

Lena sees, as I do, that no one is looking up, seeing or sensing us. The walls of the train are lined with commuters given over to complete and utter stillness. They have white wires in their ears and they bow over glowing screens.

The train moves forward under the river. I'm stopping myself from demanding seats for us. I search for an answer: what if Shakira or Lady Gaga or D'Angelo had a song called *Look Up and Find a Child!* What if these people on the train got a headphone blast of re-entering the commons, reversing the stream of information, or just opening their eyes?

And, looking up, they would simply have the dynamics of a community facing them. We would say hello and do our musical chairs trading of positions. We would be asking for the interdependency, the age-old understanding that we are ultimately raising our children together.

Will these statues be able to resist my preaching? We've had far-over-the-top preachers on the F Line before. "THIS CHILD! WITH THE EARS OF A WILD ANIMAL STICKING UP FROM HER CAP! LENA NEEDS A PLACE TO SIT!" No, that was in my mind only, I thought it — didn't shout it. Shouting in my mind.

Getting the attention of the screen-frozen is as critical to any Earth Movement, is as crucial, as the conversion of another community that doesn't see too well: cops. And just when I have THAT thought, two of New York's finest walk through the door at the Bergen Street station.

The police who arrest us on behalf of the glacier-melting bankers, and those consumers who bow to the glowing screens, they cannot continue to act on the orders of the rich. The Earth people must crack their codes, interrupt their habits and coax new behavior out of them. Use humor, music, rapping, hacking, stilt-walking, traffic-jamming. Use everything but violence to end the violence released by their compliance.

Humility check: There is no "they." Each of us is distanced from the Earth by our own culture, and we all need all of the others to bring us back. This is an urgent politics, an education, a spiritual pivot, and for many of us it will be, at first, a walk through a minefield of double-takes, embarrassment and WTF's.

The silencing that is locked down upon us in corporate culture is very strict. The repetitive choreographies are precise and unchanging. The result is the censoring of those who would be our planet criers. So now we have the culture-wide inability to shout "Emergency!" If I break into this mass hypnosis with a shout, "Give my child a seat!" I may be confronted by more subway rage, which claims lives every month in New York. And I don't want rage of any kind for my prime witness, Lena.

What did we do? We read the book we took with us from home. I read it with some difficulty, out loud and standing up. But the book is so famous and so hip hop rhythmic, I got into it and the volume of my voice rose, as it does with preachers.

The book is *The Lorax*. Our morning read is turning into an Earthalujah nonviolent but wild direct action — oh yeah! We flip the pages, holding onto the silvery ceiling handles of the F Train, unraveling the story of the Bar-ba-loots and Swomee-Swans and Truffula Trees and what were those fish called? — yes! The Humming-Fish who the Onceler forced to "walk on their fins and get woefully weary in search of some water that isn't so smeary . . . "

"What about the orangutans?! I can't believe what is happening to the orangutans!"

A young woman in a lime-green flat-top and scotch plaid skinny pants looks up from her iPhone and says evenly, "Reverend, I wasn't aware the orangutans are so near extinction. I love those lovelies with their long arms and sad expressions. I know they must be smarter than 50% of the people on this train!"

"Yes," I reply. "Their habitat is disappearing into palm oil plantation . . . and illegal logging, those old hardwood trees . . ."

And a speaker near us boomed, LADIES AND GENTLEMEN THIS IS AN IMPORTANT MESSAGE FROM THE NEW YORK PO-LICE DEPARTMENT. BE ALERT. KEEP BELONGINGS NEAR YOU AT ALL TIMES. And we both dialed the voice down simultaneously still looking at each other. Lena and I moved closer to her, edging between two — were they Mormons? — well, men in suits.

That's when Lena jumped on the young woman's lap, or tried to and sort of hit her left knee, because although the primate-lover was into it she didn't quite have the instincts for gathering a running and jumping kid into the lap area. But Lena got her place to sit, as the plaid stranger put her iPhone in her pocket in favor of the five-year-old.

Another woman, and then a man, pulled off their head-phones and signaled Thank you! to Lena and me for our performance. Lena had been singing along with the Lorax, matching my words, like a second voice in a hip hop song, because she has the whole book memorized. The cops smiled, probably parents themselves with Dr. Seuss recitations in their personal repertoire. Police can't say officially that they are Earth people, but being parents they certainly have that chance.

We look for how the Earth enters into our activism. The presence of personalities from the biosphere, in this case Dr. Seuss' wonderful animal inventions, was the Earth's cameo. The cops were a part of the story, too, the presence of armed enforcers of middle class propriety.

We pulled into the Second Avenue station and disembarked to walk the last blocks to Lena's school, she pumping with her leg out ahead on her purple scooter but always stopping on the curb and waiting for me to catch up, panting, to cross the street holding hands.

Wasn't this "breaking into public space," that time-honored noble tradition of inappropriate behavior? The performance of *The Lorax* was not a Disney production. It was physical. It was us. We performed for an audience with their ears wired to another story and we dared them to be physical and present with us. And then the orangutans swinging through the minds of the trapped commuters on that train encouraged a young woman to take off the headphones. Her brash graciousness was ringing in our hands as we waited for the light.

REPLACEMENT PLANET

DESPITE ALL THE AGONY AND CONFUSION — and death — caused by the fossil-fuel-driven globalized economy, it still has the upper hand, directing governments worldwide through banks, corporations and the very rich.

The perpetrators of this global economy have only bland names for what they do. The system has become so normalized that it has no name beyond the generic "modern economy." Mostly these bosses want to blend in and only be noticed later, after you discover you're working for them.

Those who recognize this model and loathe its destruction and disregard for life do have a name for it: "Neo-liberalism." That's a dry and confusing label, though, not much use as a way to explain things. Let's abandon it. I propose instead: *Replacement Planet*.

The Replacement Planet economy is pure and simple and deadly. It wants to replace what we used to call the Earth. Its market is everywhere. It is anything investors can find to monetize. It operates like a persistent chemical that kills and copies all it touches, saturating down to molecular particulars that cannot be seen by the naked eye, and on up to the largest aspects of the Earth, even up to the sky.

The Replacers see the Earth from the perspective of the moon, like the astronauts and that famous picture of the beautiful blue sphere, but what they see is a round ball made of a trillion products. By Replacement logic, every single thing in the world is there to be copied, rejiggered for copyright purposes, efficiencies and graphics, and then placed on the market, where it assumes value and is sold. The original beauty and usefulness becomes instantly obsolete, disposable, valueless. The point is, what does it sell for now? The sale is its only use.

Replacement Planet executives have a hard time worrying about the climate, because they believe that anything they're looking at can be made new, improved, and monetized. And I do mean *anything*, from the size of your nose to your most intimate dreams to your nation's democracy to, oh yes, that other thing — the entire Earth.

This is a neurotic, a very unwell economic model. Imagine a world where communities splinter into competing individuals or clans called corporations; where you can't give freely anymore, because all things have imminent market value. The gift economy, which is the heartbeat of any community, is an attack on the corporations' imagined profits.

This isn't an economic theory at all. It's a fundamentalist religion and a mental condition. Example: Egypt is now being sued by a French corporation because Egypt instituted a minimum wage for its people. This civic altruism, while undoubtedly saving children's lives, alters the French corporation's profit projections. The international courts, created by free trade agreements and dominated by corporations, are ruling that the corporation's planned-for net income has legal precedence over Egypt's gift to its own people. No safety net in this world is safe, because nothing on the Replacement Planet can be left outside of the market.

These zombies-in-suits even see climate change as a worthwhile revision. The melting arctic ice endangers us all, with so many of our power plants at sea level, but the melt opens up shipping lanes. Will the Replacers sue scientists for scaring people with their descriptions of methane levels in the atmosphere to match the early phase of previous extinctions? Is this attempt to save lives another illegal gift?

Rarely has world leadership been so off its nut. The suits that gather in Davos and Dotcomland, the City of London and Wall Street — they are as crazy as bedbugs. They keep calling their pixilated playground "the free market." The impact of this belief system is devastating. The way it is playing out in our lives, well, it is threatening real life.

We have not yet found the activism to slow down this killer system. Just as we have not slowed down this market's most impactful product, climate change. We have bought into the Replacement Planet so completely that most of us still don't recognize the danger we're in, back here in the world of irreplaceable, actual life.

Should we be surprised that duplicating and selling life cannot be sustained on a large scale? Will someone tell the emperor that he's stark naked?

This is why Edward Snowden is far more important as an Earth activist then, say, the Environmental Defense Fund. The system is the killer. Revealing the system for what it is, that's the mother of all campaigns. Racism, militarism, colonialism, to some extant these are many names for one thing. The system manages and murders that which it sees as outside the system, which includes all the old concepts like "democracy" and "liberty."

For those of us living on Replacement Planet, each and every product we buy trains us to normalize this bogus life.

Like all fundamentalist systems, the neo-liberal economy is violent. Replacing life is killing life. Amid all the smiling advertisements, the threat of violence is Replacement Planet's basic enforcement approach.

The natural world seems to know this. We have noticed the 200-mile-an-hour winds, the droughts, fires and floods. All around the Replacement Planet the original world is raging. The living thing called the Earth is on the move, freeing itself from the mimicry of this outer crust of products.

The Earth is shaking itself free of its proposed replacement. The Earth will control it and dissolve it in its brew of bad weather. Can we do the same with our Replacement Souls?

TO HAVE A VOICE, YOU MUST TRESPASS

WHEN A PERSON EMERGES FROM A flood or a fire, and in this heightened state of survival begins to talk about their experience, the report is often spellbinding. The tragic loss of loved ones may be weighing this soul down, and he or she may break down crying, or laugh and sigh and sit down and stare at the ground. We may be so moved by what we hear that we are changed forever. Our emotions shift, our values and our vision of change in this era of climate chaos may radically shift along with them. It's possible we will never return to the habits of the passive consumer of "news." It isn't easy to stay in the pallid mix of consumer responses if while you take in the story you're stanching a wound or spooning soup into someone's mouth.

After Hurricane Sandy we came back out into the streets and wandered wide-eyed from our terrible experience that night. We filed our unprofessional reports with strangers and neighbors, without any "research" or "production." This was the story. This was the storm moving through us. The Earth was still talking in us during those first hours, before the information was taken up and processed by the corporations for broadcast, before food and water again cost money. The tragedy was still enforcing our humanness. We were helping each other.

Listen. We'd best listen to the survivors stumbling out of the maelstrom. This is where the truth of climate change is told, coming to us with stuttering, tears and a sudden grabbing of the arm.

There is a direct line from the suffering in the storms to the focused anger of the protest. The Earth Unplugged — without the corporate mediating but the thing itself — leads to Humans Unplugged. We are still learning to do this. Experience the storm directly and walk out of all that destruction and extend the natural power we now have directly at the perpetrators of climate violence.

When in doubt, we should always return to the Earth's vantage point. Being with the victims after Sandy in Brooklyn and looking back at Goldman Sachs over there at the bottom of Manhattan, its headquarters lit up all night despite the general blackout, powered from some mysterious source they hoarded . . . the Earth's POV sees one of the principal profiteers of the crisis, glowing with triumphalism in the storm it caused! Made us want to pull that plug.

A real public communication breaks through the consumerized information and hits us with a jolt. Occupy Wall Street and Black Lives Matter had that cutting-through-it-all quality. They floored us. Black Lives Matter is still an expanding revolution, surprising us daily. Both of these movements gave us language that broke through the white noise of processed language.

The two movements began with a similar notion of activism: they both claimed a stage, a small piece of pavement in the face of power, Zuccotti Park in New York, and the sidewalk in front of the police headquarters in Ferguson. We took note of the fact that their claim of a modest square footage of public space made the surrounding entrenched powers go absolutely batshit — in the first case, Wall Street bankers, and in Ferguson, the racist police. And the waves of double-takes went out around the world. International conversations resulted. Human storms . . .

Both of these movements were accused of trespassing. *Trespassalujah!*

Let's embrace trespassing as a guiding light for our Earth activism. Property is a concept placed over the Earth, and it accumulates value while the Earth is not even entered in the books. The tradition is that the Earth is available to the property owner on a "free-use basis." It can be axed and mowed, drilled and poisoned with waste.

The biggest modern corporations are still resisting the inherent rights of the Earth, and are quick to pin the "terrorist" label on anyone who insists on Earth rights, including native people who have lived in place for thousands of years and have done so in a sustainable way.

Trespassing. Crossing a border onto territory that is claimed by another person or entity. Trespassing, a crime that in the era of climate chaos seems to give the trespasser's voice the mysterious gift of greatly amplified sound (without a permit).

In this era of militarized borders, of state-sanctioned violence toward any traveling that is not tourism, we know that we bring people home to the Earth when those borders are challenged.

And as always, the Earth is our model. Who breaks borders more thoroughly then the mother of birds that migrate thousands of miles, the subterranean old sunlight that the drills of oil companies cannot reach, and the shocking storms that whirl from continent to continent?

The Earth seems to want us to re-evolve, collide across borders — to trespass! Dear property-owner, residing in your protected abstraction: The new activist that you will desperately label a pinko anarchist nature-lover says, "Well, I'm standing on the Earth out here and I'll be standing on the Earth inside your fence too, and you and I can reflect on the fact that we are both made of the Earth. What do you say?"

Let's cross this line together. You come out, and I'll come in, and I'll come out, and you come in. It's the old in-and-out! Lovealujah! Let's practice that artful trespassing!

MAN DOWN

Monday at the deli
Talking all at once
Grabbing hands and shouting
GET HOME SAFE

Tuesday school's out early
Wanderin' through the park
Throwing shade and laughing
GET HOME SAFE

Wednesday after practice
Walking to the train
Streets alive a party
GET HOME SAFE

Working late on Thursday
Trying to stay awake
Parking lot is empty
GET HOME SAFE

Man down, brother down
Man down, brother down

Friday's family dinner
Don't be late
Can't keep your mama waitin'
GET HOME SAFE

And even Sunday
There's no restin'
Even Sunday
GET HOME SAFE

Man down, brother down
Man down, brother down
Man down, brother down
Man down, brother down

TO SAVE YOUR LIFE
IN FERGUSON

"Hands Up! Don't Shop!"
— *Black Lives Matter, on Black Friday, 2014*

IN 2014, STARTING WITH THE ERIC GARNER and Michael Brown murders in July and August, our focus turned to Black Lives Matter. The African American singers in our choir led the way, especially the mothers with their unshakeable emotion. (And this focus is ongoing. I'm writing while on tour with Neil Young, and every night we sing out a long series of names of the black men and women killed by the police, casting a thoughtful silence on the rock crowd.) Our work against Monsanto's toxins ran parallel to our work against deadly police violence, and the campaigns vibrated alongside each other like the two tines of a tuning fork. We would sing a song about the Earth and then a song about the police, one after the other. We began to see that the violence of bullets and the violence of toxins have the same source, and therefore must have the same solution. They can each be stopped by the same peace.

We came to understand that Earth Justice and Human Justice must ring out as one. It happened one night during a performance in a Walmart parking lot.

Earlier that year we had decided to plan a trip to the dark heart of Monsanto. In the spirit of that activism in which ordinary living is staged in public, as inspired by Gezi, Zuccotti, Tahrir, and the Indignados of Puerta del Sol in Madrid, we would eat our Thanksgiving dinner at the front gate of Monsanto's World Headquarters in Missouri.

Oh that company. The folks that brought you Agent Orange, honeybee-killing neonicotinoids and cancer-causing glyphosate pesticides, suicide seeds and the corruption of the EPA. Damn! The evil makes me type harder!

We raised $25,000 for the bus trip that spring of 2014, so that we could take the whole choir to Monsanto in November. Then Michael Brown was killed and Daryl Wilson wasn't even indicted, and Eric Garner, and Tamir Rice, and John Crawford, and on and on. The country's newfound ability to notice police murders cascaded down upon us.

It turns out that the rambling Monsanto headquarters campus is located in Creve Coeur, Missouri. Right next door to Ferguson.

It was a 16-hour overnight trip, with two drivers from a charter company taking shifts at the wheel. We got there the next day and found rooms at a hotel near the St. Louis airport. It was fun for four-year-old Lena, because the hotel had a sort of cheap-ass Vegas quality, lots of stairs and landings, bridges over a lobby pool.

We took a nap, and then piled into the bus and set off to Monsanto. Suddenly the police called. Savi took it. "We understand you're coming to Monsanto. We'd like to make this a good experience for you." Had they hacked our emails? They were waiting for us when we pulled up.

About a hundred of us sang and preached and prayed in the snow that day in front of Monsanto. There were anti-GMO and pro-Earth enthusiasts, faithful who had driven all the way from Omaha and Chicago and Denver to join us. We gathered first in a local park and gabbed up a storm, talking about progressive campaigns we'd shared and finding mutual friends in our memories of activist life.

The St. Louis Earth-lovers were so generous. They navigated for us, explaining the nuances of area police as we marched along the road for about two miles; they joined us in remembering Selma and Ferguson and simultaneously the suicides of South Asian farmers, caught in Monsanto credit schemes.

Our culinary singers had prepared the Thanksgiving dinner at a local shelter for the homeless. They roasted the beets, potatoes, squash, parsnips, carrots and sweet potatoes, with lots of garlic and onions, and we steamed the kale, collards and chard, and there was delicious stuffing plus the all-important vegan stuffing option, and then there were the pies, and the meal was spread before us on swaying tables over the snow-covered ground.

The afternoon of testimonials and good cheer became colder and colder, hard by the fortresslike Monsanto gate-sign, which sported the sprig of green that is Monsanto's unlikely logo.

Police loomed around us, silhouettes in the snow glowing behind them. They watched us from the middle distance with benign faces when we could see them in the glare. We sent hot cider to the cops with the children, and they couldn't refuse that, waving at us with smiles.

Our radical holiday partners testified, and I preached and the choir sang the "Monsanto Is The Devil" song for our goodbye to these citizens who fight for food safety. And maybe the cops heard our song, too:

> *Monsanto is the Devil*
> *Pretends he's a scientist*
> *The pest we need for this predator*
> *Evolution with a kiss*
> *That's where you and I come in*
> *The human super bug*
> *With Mother Earth's instructions*
> *Save your seeds with love*
> *Devil Monsanto, listen up!*

Finally we succumbed to the cold, got back in our bus and immediately told the driver, "Take us to Ferguson."

There could be no other next place. We drove to Michael Brown's memorial site on Canfield drive, to hold hands in front of the flowers, sneakers and teddy bears covered with snow. We stood there in silence, not singing or saying anything. Small groups of people here and there along the street stopped, lost in thought. Then we felt someone's presence. There, like a smiling, soft statue in the light of the streetlamp, was Mama Cat.

Her full name is Cathy Daniels. A woman with stillness in her bearing but energy in her stride, she easily commandeered us to help her load food from a nearby apartment into her van. Soon our bus was en route to St. Luke's Church, where a hullabaloo that mixed radical rage with holiday cheer welcomed us. We took Mama Cat's food down to the kitchen, along with our own leftover organic fare, mixing it in with the soul food on the counter.

The basement room was packed with Ferguson families. And it was crowded with sympathetic activists from around the world, and lots of European media.

In that low-yellow-ceilinged church basement we were at close quarters with this swirling humanity, kids shouting and grandparents smiling and families breaking into song. It felt like a labyrinth collapsing because of some agreement. What do we all understand here? Everyone was looking into everyone else's face. Mama Cat was in and out of the steamy kitchen. Tables of food fronted on the mad rush of this morally roused community.

The chattering, laughing, buzzing in the air . . . I felt something there. It was unmistakable. It was the feeling I had in Union Square after 9/11. This was the Madison, Wisconsin rotunda in the spring of 2011. This was the opening night of *Angels in America*. Everyone is interested because change is promised by a delicious tension in the air.

The microphone went from old aunties to preachers to children to choir leaders, testifying and testifying again. Our music director, Nehemiah, was channeling his church-kid self from Jackson, Mississippi, having taken over an old organ in the corner. Delighted singers rotated by him, each with a gospel song, all of which he knew, throwing his head back and singing big. Everyone sang "This Little Light of Mine," and time stood still with that sweet civil rights anthem.

Then came Dragonfly's passionate testimony about Aiyana Stanley-Jones, the seven-year-old killed while sleeping on a couch next to her grandmother when Detroit police knocked down their front door in a night raid. (There has never been an indictment.)

Let's take a moment to regard the courage of this little, previously unknown town of Ferguson. Of all the cities in the United States with 60,000 population, the city with the highest number of black males absent from daily life because of death, flight or illness: Ferguson, Missouri. In 2015 it was revealed that the 95%-white police department had been running a racist racketeering scam, tracking families and individuals, entrapping citizens in parking ticket and traffic fine nightmares with loan sharks working to deepen the debt.

How did these black teenagers claim ownership of a patch of sidewalk, and how did they cling to it for those long late-summer nights, all the way from Michael Brown's death on August 9 and on into October, to finally see their story rise to the top of the news? How is it that they were ready for this? They acted as if they already knew what worldwide fame was.

That night in the basement of St. Luke's the people built up and built up the delirium for the demand that the killing stop. The call and response from teenagers, toothless grandmothers, hip-hoppers — I sat there mesmerized. I'm still sitting here, amazed.

These people had emerged from truly intimidating violence. These were ecstatic survivors. And I still wonder, will environmentalists ever have such intensity? We have no choice.

Cop cars were lighting up the mesh windows along the top of the church basement walls, red and blue lights flashing, as we climbed the steps into the night. We crossed the pavement into the parking lot with the cops beaming their lights through the side alleys, but we carried in us the experience of that basement, Mama Cat's food and the testimony of a town. We were still singing "This Little Light of Mine." We knew where we were going because our destination had been whispered from person to person across the basement, a secret call-and-response under the song.

Now we drove in a caravan to the on-ramp and up onto the freeway. I noticed the menace of night in the north suburbs of St. Louis. We were on the elevated interstate, and the darkness below was uninhabitably lightless, like some science fiction planet covered with abysses. The only islands of light were strip malls. This is the fate of American cities, designed by dollars and cynical inertia, with the citizens of this dystopia chased by cops on elevated strips of concrete.

Our destination was a Walmart about ten miles away. We parked along the edges of the lot and walked toward the familiar Walmart logo, toward a wall of National Guard soldiers and cops with dogs, hastily lining themselves up. They had given us an uncomfortable police escort on the highway, then followed us down the off-ramp and parked behind the big box. We walked through the electronic doors in twos and threes, through the gauntlet of police mixed with store security, deep into the heart of the fluorescent store.

We gathered in the electronics entertainment section, with row upon row of Katy Perry on flatscreen TVs. And we waited there, in the tension with a touch of a party. Some of us pretended to shop, which felt like a really weird pantomime, picking up an item and reading the label, then thoughtfully placing it back on the shelf. Incredible! How can anyone shop here! Ever!

Then here come our young leaders through the aisle, shouting HANDS UP! DON'T SHOP!

We circled within the store, our hands aloft in surrender—to what? We walked in mock surrender to the products; to the hypnotic products that finally failed to distract us from the violence in our daily lives.

We broke the deal of Consumerism: we are supposed to walk into that colorful fog of products and their advertising and submit to it, and dedicate our lives to Black Friday grosses. That was our patriotic obligation. The cops with their dogs seemed startled that we were breaking the faith. It was as if they were thinking, "Are you rejecting the American way of life? And what are you saying with this 'Hands Up! Don't Shop!' That if you shop, you'll drop dead? What are you saying? The products are bullets? Is this a joke?"

No, not a joke. The HANDS UP! DON'T SHOP! theme for this Thanksgiving weekend was introduced by the Ferguson coalition of preachers. Strike Big Retail for justice. Things got more charged as we walked faster. For these Ferguson citizens this was like a hundred of such nights. The difference this night was that racism was tied to Consumerism.

Our HANDS UP! DON'T SHOP! built in intensity, overcoming the Muzak of the products. Then about 200 chanting anti-shoppers, including the punk gospel singers in the Stop Shopping Choir, moved toward the front of the store, back through the flummoxed cops and soldiers to the parking lot in front of the electronic glass doors. We then turned in a circle and faced them.

Then came the high point of the demonstration of teachable courage. The citizens of Ferguson faced the line of riot-cops. The violence of that militarized wall of humanity would have impressed most of us. But for the Ferguson people, with the practice of scores of nights of this, the tradition they had developed together, it released them into a point blank dance-a-thon.

I've never seen anything like it. They took a breath, walked to the center of the line of police, and stared them down. The sentries of white power and property, back-lit by the infamous big box, were gonna get some new culture.

One by one the people of Ferguson rolled out their shows. You could call what they did performance, backed by a mad church chorus of revelers across the pavement. You could call it a desperate lunge at freedom and safety.

As with the passing of the microphone in the church basement, everyone took a turn. For some, it was a dance, a frenetic dance, inches from the cops and their dogs. For others, older people, the performance was a sermon to these childish big brutes, but often the sermonettes were surprisingly gentle. When one of the cops seemed to lose his concentration, he got a lecture from a grandmotherly woman, "You pay attention, your full attention. You need to show some respect and learn something tonight, young man! You've got to learn to stop killing! That's hard work for you, and for me, too."

For the mostly young whites in uniform, they got a hell of a civics lesson about responsibility, peace and safety. Preacher sermonizers, hip hop reciters, teenage girls singing, and then back to the preachers again, the show continued on, punctuated by the usual announcement that we were on private property and that if we did not leave we would be arrested. This kind of pontificating would be met by energetic derision and another spinning, blurring dance.

We felt a common fierceness as we helped maintain a rhythmic bed of sound with *We Can't Breathe!* and *Hands Up!* In the bonding together, there were implacable emotions. Above all there was anger, but also there was sorrow, with the names of the dead always surfacing. The name of Michael Brown was cycled back through the tumult, like an exploding afterword to his funeral.

Everyone had the job of making a world with his or her own body. Everyone had the few inches and feet around them, a space to whip into something personally unforgettable, just beyond the reach of the German shepherds. After half an hour the lawmen had stiffened into monuments; their eyes had been glaring at the beginning, but after the performances went on a while the police began to lose any quality at all. Their effort to stand their ground became an opaque deadness.

The impact of these testifying citizens, dancing and singing and shouting, was so fierce, so like hammers that stopped just before the nail, inches from the wide eyes of Walmart's defenders — it suddenly became clear to us that *these Ferguson residents feel safer doing this than in their everyday lives in this city.*

This terrifying face-off was much safer than daily life under the law and order of those police. Yes, better to be here, in the energy field of this ferocity, freezing the white cops in place, in public, with media all around, in the center of this stolen commons — safer to be here than to go back home and try to have a family life on a street with trigger-happy official violence at the ready. Don't go back to wondering if the children will make it home. (There were a lot of mothers in the Walmart parking lot that night, and a fair amount of children too, even as we approached midnight.)

One middle-aged woman in a silver Oakland Raiders windbreaker and red tights embarked on a dance that we will never forget. She mounted a performance that crossed an Alvin Ailey modern dance solo with some kind of precision seizure.

She whirled and fizzed and screamed. The woman left "Stop killing us!" hanging in the air before the wall of cops. Some of the younger ones stared dully in disbelief, or unexpected new belief. It seemed inevitable that they would arrest her, but she was transforming into a flashing liquid, sweating against the shiny fascist crewcuts and hat brims, the badges and ribbons, with their guts hanging out.

This spitting screaming angering and sorrowing woman was fire in the air. She stayed within millimeters of the bodies of the Ferguson police. Their faces were covered with amazement at the motion of this black woman.

The police captain tried to break the spell. He announced again: "You are on private property, you must leave . . ." and "You are interrupting the legitimate shoppers . . ." and "You are violating the Ferguson curfew . . ." But she pinned these words to his mouth. The recitation of laws was less and less convincing in the face of the prosecution by this spinning dancer.

The people we had joined in the basement of that church went on into the night, a caravan of dancers-on-police. Off to the next Walmart, Target, Macy's — safer to keep on performing — on into the morning on that YOU CAN NOW SHOP FOR 24 HOURS Black Friday. We had to bow out, and we hugged them all and thanked them, told them that we believed that they were changing everyone with their commitment, but we needed to return to New York first thing in the morning.

The young Ferguson uprisers and the reverends and the dancing woman, they graciously thanked us in return and let us go. As we drove from the parking lot we could see them turn back to the stage that they would not leave, for the next week and month and perhaps years. The silhouettes of the sentries, with the blinding bright shopping displays behind them, waited for this act of citizenship, which they could not arrest or shoot. The Ferguson resistance that we all depend on started up all over again.

We knew that we had met this rare thing: radical Americans in open revolt. If many of us had questioned whether we can ever be radical Americans again, as we were in the historic uprisings that won our freedoms, the Ferguson citizens left us without a doubt. Yes, there is a way to escape the chains of consumerism and the security state. We can say that this is a time to be radical Americans again and we can know that it is possible. It is all we can possibly do.

"Hands Up! Don't Shop!" opened a door of perception for us in the Church of Stop Shopping. Ferguson confirmed our long-held intuition about the racism of the all-shopping culture of consumerism. We have seen the overlap of the two systems, Militarism and Consumerism — and we saw in the practice of Ferguson's activism the confirmation of that duo of Devils.

The police of Ferguson had justified their racism by turning all encounters with Ferguson residents into profit centers. The volunteerism of the old neighborhood beat cop was replaced by the monetizing of every stop of black citizens by white police. The citizenry became involuntary consumers. They paid, and paid and paid. But what were they buying? They were consumers and they were consumed, like a forest that's harvested down to pavement and rusty cyclone fencing.

Over the years, the police found that they could presume criminal behavior, and then create tickets, make arrests, and build a database of potential client–criminals. The further they penetrated the homes of their constituency, the more crime they could develop. They were ready with scores of charges. The bails were high, the jails full, and black families were constantly in court. It was creative and satisfying for the police in that macho way — and it was guided by their fear of the black population.

Ferguson's most famous danger for citizens was the risk in crossing into public space, dramatized forever by the murder of Michael Brown on August 9, 2014. To "leave home while black" was to encounter a withering police presence. And as long as the police crimes did not receive legal review, it followed that more and more of regular community life could be monetized, once it was written up as criminal behavior. And so racism turned into big retail. The police and the Walmart behind them that we faced that Black Friday night are both institutions of Consumerism.

In the end, the federal government determined that what the police had been doing was racketeering. The feds pushed out Ferguson's police leadership in a series of public firings. But this racketeering is a miniature of the economy of the larger United States. Ferguson illustrates the virulence of consumerism. Guns and ads. Toxic chemicals and bullets. The oppressive monoculture — the concoction of sales and arrests — is labeled "Freedom" and "Democracy" and "America."

A new generation of young people is arriving in this world, and in large numbers they are radical environmentalists in a seemingly natural way. They recognize the legacy the white power structure is leaving them. They see what Consumerism and Militarism are. They have no patience for racketeering police, handing out tickets in a form of unlegislated taxation, or for the corporate versions of this — student debt, fraudulent mortgages, privacy attacks and surveillance, environmental pollution, profit-taking prisons. When the young come into the world from families that are not sufficiently hypnotized, the machine begins to break.

A New York example of this is a simple demand by the youth living in the Bronx projects — they want access to the Bronx River, and that the river be clean enough for them to go swimming and boating. This turned everything upside down, including the whole system of law and order in that benighted borough. Earth justice pushes the police back, as citizens grow green space and govern themselves, free of intimidation.

The youth of Ferguson, and their sisters and brothers who crossed the country to be with them from Oakland and

Watts, New York and Chicago, know that the negotiations with killers can only start when the killers know that shooting at us, imprisoning us, is useless — *that no violence can stop us.*

There is a fistful of messages for environmentalists from these young teachers in Ferguson. Don't cooperate with a killing culture. Resist. Don't let false advertising confuse you. Don't believe the hype!

Earthers need to rap that phrase with Public Enemy. Carbon dioxide and methane and nitrous oxide pour into the air when plants and animals are killed, yes, but we also poison the Earth when we take away the freedoms of ordinary citizens. The flowering life of a human being — that is the Earth, too.

The Ferguson citizens tore open a safe place in the claustrophobic air of Consumerism and Militarism. They danced open a safe place. The totalizing system that controls us could not hold them. It does not have to hold us, either. And it cannot hold the Earth.

AMARANTH, ACTION HERO

THE AMARANTH PLANT IS CALLED BAD NAMES by Monsanto and the journalists who go along with the corporation's press releases. They try to get the *New York Times* to call it "Superweed" or "Pigweed." The befuddling genius of amaranth comes down to this: it has re-organized its desires to outmaneuver the genetic engineering of Monsanto. Amaranth plants *like* the taste of Monsanto's franchise toxin: glyphosate. Amaranth eats Roundup, the most popular herbicide in the world. Amaranth eats glyphosate-drenched cornfields with gustatory pleasure.

Amaranth can grow three inches a day to a height of seven feet . . . an Avenging Angel! Amaranth is a flourishing citizen of the modern world. In the original Greek, it means "unfading flower." That's an understatement. Yes, it doesn't fade. Amaranth is a beautiful plant, with greens and reds mixing in its leaves. It is a long-time serving on the plate of those who dine on wild edibles and has a long history with native peoples. It is especially identified with the people of the Yucatan, but its seeds have traveled toward El Norte as it has evolved its powerful appetites. It is the natural food parallel, in its travel and change, to its world-conquering counterpart — the corn plant. The two co-exist to this day in their old, more benign forms in Mexico, but have grown to do battle, the natural against the industrial, in the fields of Monsanto.

Monsanto has no answer to amaranth, and won't. It was always predicted by opponents of the genetic engineering of plants that the corporations would be unable to overcome the evolutionary powers of the natural world that surrounds them.

The Earth is a living being that wants to survive. It is life — it is life serving life. This global yearning gives amaranth a special mission, and a guiding intelligence. The uncanny tactics of evolution will overwhelm grinning actors on the website graphics. Monsanto's executives labor under the cock-eyed optimism of corporate expansion. Such a belief casts nature as passive and even inert, a backdrop for the heroism of money. This is Monsanto's death warrant. The life that waits within the unknown needs Monsanto's death, and this apocalypse is proceeding apace at this very moment. You'd best join the parade!

Monsanto is trying to invent a seed that flourishes quickly, like a fire-works display, under conditions of extreme drought. The desertification that industrial agriculture is creating with its toxicity is its indispensable business solution, its profit center. Sales from this monoculture will expand as the climate (and all wildness) dies. But out in the fields of life — unknowable to the fossil fuel-manipulating chemists — amaranth is ready for any profit-driven adjustments with its out-flanking maneuvers.

Amaranth, a member of a famous family of plants and flowers with some 70 species, has in its secret life a genius for invention. It seems likely that amaranth will have varieties ready for droughts, for fires, and even a fresh-water seaweed for the Mississippi floods that are another of the Earth's responses to the industrial agriculture in the Midwest.

Amaranth is beautiful and formidable. The amaranth presence at the Monsanto headquarters in St. Louis would be noticed by the gardeners, who would respond quickly with their weed-killer, and inform agriculture and parks officials. It would raise the eyebrows of genetic engineers from the St. Louis laboratories, and word would get around among the crop-duster pilots. Amaranth is legendary. Amaranth has the evolutionary ability to follow the engineering upstream, so to speak.

No one really knows what drives such explicit countermoves to artificial life — yes, amaranth seems to have a job in enforcement for the Earth. Monsanto executives carry the unique human chauvinism, the opinion that only the human species (in a business suit) has intelligence But the Earth made us. The Earth maketh and the Earth taketh away.

There comes the day when the Monsanto board of directors will meet at the headquarters of the company's global operations, in the suburbs of St. Louis, Missouri. The group of millionaires from throughout the corporate world will take their seats around a long hardwood table, deeply varnished, glowing with mysterious rivulets of color, like a long polished agate. The boardroom in the upper reaches of the office building has a rarified hush. The wealthy executives chat quietly in their tailored suits.

The twelve board members pull their leather chairs forward. The President of the board clears his throat. They are about to find a way to distort their shrinking earnings and create another export of corporate boosterism to the shareholders and analysts, yet another rendition of Monsanto's billions-making duet of "Better Living Through Chemistry" and "Oh What a Beautiful Morning, Oh What a Beautiful Day." One of the executives turns, and the blood drains from his face. Another glances at the window and does a double-take. The board is frozen there: the Apocalypse of Monsanto has begun.

The amaranth plant is at the window. In fact, many amaranths are there, the building is cloaked in them. They love the taste of glyphosate-coated glass. That damn pigweed! The scene in the window resembles a greenhouse of amaranths, rooting and climbing. And there's more — neonicotinoid-eating killer honey bees, and superhumans evolved to find strength in Agent Orange. This is a whole ecosystem of bitter survivors. There are so many of them! The board members are crouching beneath the table, a little like school kids in a 1950s education film about what to do if the Russians attack. It's duck and cover for the Monsanto leadership. Suddenly, the glass breaks . . .

THE FABULOUS
UNKNOWN

THE EARTH TELLS US TO TOUCH, learn, grow, change, respond to others and never stop the music. Get that power from dancing in the streets, that collective joy, and then turn to face the Devil again. The strongest human communication is love, because love makes life.

You see, I'm imagining our evolution will re-create us as much more powerful Earth citizens. The Earth made our organism this way, after all — we are at the heart of evolution when we actively love. What am I saying?! This feels like Walt Whitman plus direct action!

Then there is this rub: We don't have any idea how love works. All the songs are about love but no one knows what it is. Something about love makes us fools singing at the moon. I will crawl across broken glass on all fours with your underwear clenched in my teeth and not know why.

Here's a key: love is unknowable. With love we are entering the Fabulous Unknown. And you cannot replace what you don't know.

One of the most revealing demonstrations of the horrible result of "knowing everything" comes to us from Monsanto. That corporation believes it knows all there is to know about life on Earth, and cannot imagine there's anything at all

that's not replaceable. That is, all life on Earth can be geneti-
cally "mapped" and then copyrighted and owned, turned into
a product for sale — and possible profit. This explains why
Monsanto's cultists don't pray to the Earth, or sing to it, or
love it.

In the Church of Stop Shopping we know the love is
unknowable and we believe that the Fabulous Unknown is a
wondrous thing that is at the heart of all activism. This cannot
be copyrighted or sold, love cannot be known or replaced.

Always start a new nonviolent direct action with mysterious love. Not strategy, not policy, not theory. Start with love.
Kiss and then follow the waves that go out from your lips —
fly with it, like the bees. Our experience is that nothing can
ever embarrass you with this approach. Old social condition-
ing falls away. Constructs like ego and fear and the Replacers'
laws and products — forgotten. Your activism will buzz with
life. You will fly to justice!

Replacement Bees
Let's consider the honeybee. The honeybee has partnered
with humans since the mists of pre-history, sharing its honey
with us the way that lovers share the honey of their bodies.
The honeybee is a symbol of love in many of our songs, and
it smiles at us in our children's books. There are more bees on
royal family coats of arms than lions, tigers, or bears, oh my!
The bee is here with us, on this planet called the Earth.

The honeybee is threatened now. Forty percent of all the
bees in the United States — honeybees, as well as thousands
of wild bees — perished in 2014. Most beekeepers blame
neonicotinoids.

The neonicotinoid pesticides, or "neonics," are a best-selling insect-killer, manufactured and sold under various names by corporations like Monsanto, Syngenta and Bayer. And just as it sounds, this class of poison is a fierce version of nicotine.

Neonics are neuropathic chemicals, and they short-circuit the sophisticated navigation system that directs the bees from the hive to the discovery of distant flowers and back to the hive again. This tragedy is intensely sad. The bees are spiraling off, lost, flying vainly till they die of exhaustion miles away. They must feel a kind of loneliness. Do bees have feelings? Do they have the kind of feelings that incite me to sing B.B. King's "The Thrill Is Gone"? Who knows. We can't prove that the bees' sorrow is like our own.

But we can use our own sorrow-turned-into-anger to stop the killing of the bees. It seems that Monsanto, Syngenta and Bayer's plan is to replace the honey bee, because the bee can't keep pace with the rising potency of their poisons. How can we allow them to end such life, to replace it with profit? Especially when we know it's impossible — you can't replace a mystery with a product.

Let us muse for a moment on the flight of Apis mellifera, the honeybee. I'll choose my awed words carefully. Let's start with the finding of just-bloomed flowers by the bee that scouts for the hive. The dancing language of the scout bees, the communicating of a map to a new source of flowery nutrition miles from the hive, is miraculous. It's as if the Holy Spirit became a swarm, and the swarm broke up into many beings, each meandering purposefully across the land, spreading the intelligence of the original sprit.

The scout bee travels miles away from the hive, mapping out the land. On her flight back from her reconnaissance journey she is seen by sentry bees, and the hive is alerted. The scout prepares her report. The news will come in a performance for the buzzy audience inside the swirly ball of paper that we call the hive. Yes, they actually have stages inside those swirly gray paper medicine balls.

She dances. Let us count the ways. She emits pheromone-like perfumes. She drums with her feet and vibrates her abdomen under the high-hat of her wings, which beat at 70 times a second. The choreographic line of her dance on the hive floor is a super-precise compass needle pointing to the flower miles away. Soon hundreds of bees fly off, knowing exactly where to go.

This literally is a language. Entomologists accept that the scout bees' dancing report is a language. For years, human scientists resisted this idea because our chauvinist species only wants intelligence in animals to manifest in cuties like dolphins, chimps and elephants. But now the intelligence of the hive must be included in this pantheon.

It has been discovered that this map-making dance, performed inside the hive and affectionately called the "waggle dance" by entomologists, triangulates the position of the sun with the spinning of the Earth and the location of the hive. The scout bee makes a far better map than any kind of GPS.

Let's go deeper into this. Researchers recently noted that after the first waggle dance is completed, and that audience departs for the distant flowers, then another stage will be prepared for another dance in another part of the hive. When the scout bee prepares her report for this second audience, her geometry changes. Her language changes. Why?

Well, say that the first dance-report took 20 minutes. To begin her second report she makes an adjustment in her second dance, adjusts her percussion, her buzzing melodies, and pheromones and angling dance to account for the precise change in the relative positions of the Earth and sun and hive. Honeybeelujah!

Monsanto employees and contractors who might read this, take note: We keep finding out how incredible the life of the bee is, but the slow coming into the known, into human knowledge, suggests that what we don't know and may never know goes as deep into mystery as the stars, or love, or death. Does this impact your impulse to copy and improve on nature? In the case of the honeybees, it seems that what is unknown to humans has been running the whole show.

The Earth cannot be replaced because it is mostly unknown to us. We can only extract, kill, copy and replace that which is clearly understood. Meanwhile, 98% of the Earth looms around us unknown, as we murder plants and animals and each other.

We have a chorus of elders who are singing the song of the unknown to us. Zora Neale Hurston's cherry tree blossoming in *Their Eyes Were Watching God*; Rachel Carson's undulating seaweed and somersaulting shells of the Maine tidepools; Edward Abbey hovering over the Colorado River as he starts Earth First!; Federico García Lorca in Spain writing his *Deep Song*; Chief Joseph telling us that "the Earth is the mother of all people, and all people should have equal rights upon it." These wise ones perceive the unknown. They stand on the horizon of what they can sense and understand, look out into creation, and sing those words that guide us.

There is activist power in unknowable nature. We want to save the bees, of course, because we revere their mysterious whirling hives; how the thousands of bees pursue the good of the hive; how these creatures hover and buzz, making decision after decision, the endless interlocking moves, the mass making its survival.

We feel a swarming coming on. We are in Monsanto's lobby, on their roof, at their stockholders' convention, in their mind. We are creating the miracle. We're emitting the pheromones. Our wings are beating at 70 times a second. And the former Blackwater USA officials that Monsanto hires for security, who study us, must know that we have our own waggle dance — we are designed by the sun and the Earth and our brothers and sisters in the hive. And at the end of their notes in the file they keep on us, the corporate cops must add that we activists are unknowable, too.

FLYING

I've got apocalypse fatigue, my honeybee and me
Where's my home hive gone
Where's my sweet, sweet tree?

A thousands flowers touching me
They know I know the queen
They touch the hive through me
They see the tree in a dream

Circle around, circle around, circle around
Circle around, circle around

I carry sticky gold dust
Buzzing on a broken breeze
I'm spiraling off shore
And now I'm lost at sea

Oh you can't go home again
You can't go home
No you can't go home again
You can't go home

ROBOBEES
VS. HONEYBEES
IN THE IVY LEAGUE

RIGHT NOW, HARVARD SCIENTISTS ARE BUSILY designing one of the Pentagon's wildest dreams, the "Robobee," a tiny drone that will use the flying techniques of the honey bee. The name of Harvard's well-financed Robobee facility is the Micro-Robotics Lab, a part of the School of Engineering and Applied Sciences. The Lab is housed in a four-story building on Harvard's campus in Cambridge, deep in the bricks-and-vines gentility of the Ivy League. In April 2014, the Church of Stop Shopping began a series of spiritual invasions, the singers full of Honeybeelujah, walking under the stately old elms from the Harvard Natural History Museum toward the infernal laboratories of the Frankenbee.

You've got to hand it to them, this robot-in-the-making has a pretty good name — with a sort of sentimental, goofy, Disneyesque sound. This is one reason this robot effort has gotten such good press. There is a loveable quality and the name rolls off the tongue with a smile. It is both product and mascot: the Robobee.

The Robobee would fly like a bee. And that is saying a lot. The flight of the bee is dazzling, stopping on a dime, flying off in a new direction, effortlessly adjusting to different speeds, then plunging directly into flowers. In the case of the Western honeybee, we see a complete mastery of the air on display as they fly from flower to flower, sometimes more than a thousand flowers on each trip.

Despite its staff of scores of researchers and engineers, and its budget of over $10 million per annum, in the Robobee Lab's five-year history it has not created a flying machine that can fly freely for any distance. They have failed to miniaturize the power system, and the stick-like robot still needs a charge cord. You can't fly to a thousand flowers, or bomb a thousand villages, dragging a wire that you need to plug in . . .

Oh, did I mean to say "bomb a thousand villages?" Have I misspoken? Am I unfair to see this level of Evil? No, the Pentagon's DARPA program (Defense Advanced Research Project Agency, creators of the internet!) publicly stated its plans for militarized hummingbirds, dragonflies, bats, and bees as early the late 1950s, hosting conferences and academic publications. Today, researchers are being engaged to create — in DARPA-speak — "a new class of algorithms to enable small, unmanned aerial vehicles to quickly navigate a labyrinth of rooms, stairways and corridors or other obstacle-filled environments without a remote pilot." (I invite readers not to think of their own homes at this moment.)

Thus our activism against the Robobee Lab is in the role of peacemakers. We know that the war machine is behind this. We know this because we "follow the money," even though the head scientist at the lab, the DARPA fellow Dr. Robert J. Wood, downplays the lab's connection to Pentagon coffers.

Increasingly DARPA seems to want to harness the

capabilities of nature. The Battlefield Illusions program, for example, involves "weaponized hallucinations." This is stealth technology taken to the next step. On an afternoon in a contested village somewhere in the Middle East, an enemy soldier is thinking that all he sees are clouds and birds, and a lazy, stray dog. I'll leave the rest of that battle to your imagination. Fighting the Americans of the future, you will have reason to be suspicious of a cloud of mosquitoes, that owl hooting at night, and the squirrel on the roof of your tent.

DARPA's model of the future has a terrifying ideal. The Earth will have American drones penetrating the natural ecosystems, with local species carrying cameras or ordinance, easily dispatched in flocks toward the object of our violence, using the camouflage that the natural world provides. And so we designed our action against the Robobee Lab in the belief that it is a military program of this horrifying model of a future where the natural world becomes indistinguishable from the American attack.

At the top of the list posted on the Robobee Lab's website of possible uses for their invention sits the imposing promise, "Mechanical Pollination." They call this a humanitarian use. They like the idea of replacing the honeybee with smartbees that are programmed by computers to efficiently buzz in a straight line, directly to the target flowers. The cost benefit of the natural meandering of the bees does not make sense to the corporate or Pentagon-sponsored scientists.

In the Church of Stop Shopping we are straightforwardly Luddite on the whole question of the Robobee. You can't replace the honeybee, and you shouldn't try. We respect that meandering, even if we can't explain why it's important. No, we should not be trying to replace the bee; we should be saving it. The honeybee is the human being's oldest food-making partner, after all, and it is now a threatened species. Its population has plunged in recent years by nearly half. This is an emergency, and it is what fuels our singing and our preaching.

The Communications Officers who tried to talk to us as we entered the Robobee Lab insisted that they were very sorry that the honeybee is disappearing. They love honeybees, too. Who doesn't? But, alas, they were helpless to do anything about it. They said this while they stared at the singers of the Stop Shopping Choir. We were covered with five-inch-long bees, dozens on each of us, clusters of them on our arms and shoulders as we began to sing to the scientists, *"I got apocalypse fatigue, my honeybee and me . . . "*

Seven hundred honeybees made of faux fur, with plastic diamond eyes and pipe-cleaner legs, emerged slowly from our home, mostly by Savitri's handiwork. The Stop Shoppers did help her now and again with weekend bee-making at our dining room table, but our director insisted on her own precision, and the outcome proved how important that was. They are scarily real yet unreal. They are an homage to the real thing, but over the top, too, flamboyant drag-queens of a bee.

The body of the bee is made of dark gold fur, and it is shaped to a point by brushed-on laminate that hardens so the fur takes on the classic shape of a bee's abdomen. This is then wrapped in black wire to make the bee's stripes. Around the head the fur flares out like the mane of a little lion. The wings are made of a fine mesh, held in shape by an outline of gold wire. The face has the facets of a black diamond bauble, and the proboscis sticks out with black pipe cleaner.

The cloud of bees on our bodies as we crossed into the "contested space" of the Robobee Lab was a fierce thing to behold. And good on the scientists and their Communications Officers for not calling security. Maybe they felt that the bee dolls signaled some kind of camaraderie.

After all, these corporatized scientists are making a bee, and we have made our bee, too. And we are both claiming to do it out of admiration and love of this third bee, the real one. Their weaponized idea for the bee is taking five years and counting, and our 700 totem-dolls took ten weeks. The real one evolved, along with its 25,000 fellow bee species, for eons.

As we clothed ourselves in bees, and visited beekeepers in Europe and the U.S. during our touring, we began to fall in love the way beekeepers do. Gradually we could feel the emotions of the hive. It didn't surprise us when we heard about the bees' sorrow. Honey bees will attend their beekeeper's funeral. They actually slow down their buzz and mourn. The tradition is to leave a strip of the dead beekeeper's clothing near the hive, and then take it to the memorial with the bees trailing in the sky. In the Church of Stop Shopping, we feel on faith that the long years of evolution have blessed the honeybees with something very complex. Let's call it a soul.

We believe this on faith but we also keep running into bees who seem to know what we're up to. When we cover ourselves with Savi's bee dolls, the real bees descend on us. It might be something about our costumes, the synthetic material we pin the bee dolls to might have something to do with it. Are we like big activist flowers?

Or do they like our harmonies? Are we making a superstorm-size waggle dance? Do they know we are singing about them? They like to listen, it seems. It's happened in Edinburgh, in Times Square and at Harvard, too. If we sing the following lyrics, bees alight on our shoulders:

> *I got apocalypse fatigue, my honeybee and me*
> *Where's my home hive gone, where's my sweet sweet tree?*
>
> *A thousand flowers touching me, they know I know the queen,*
> *They touch the hive through me, they see my tree in a dream.*
>
> *Circle around, circle around, circle around . . .*

We gently disinvited the real bees from our shoulders when we left the great lawns of Harvard and entered the Robobee Lab. At that point we had to represent them, perform on their behalf. This was the plan as we walked in the door, our eyes darting around, watchful for security. We were a gospel choir covered with swarms of our church-made bees, singing up the steps toward the drone labs.

We brought information about our "Monsanto Is The Devil" work. We carried a big basket of the many kinds of fruits and vegetables pollinated by the bees. And we had our media friends in tow, Elizabeth Kolbert from the *New Yorker*, Kaelyn Forde from Al Jazeera and Anna Merlan from the *Village Voice*. Teddy Tam, one of the church's film-makers, had the camera. John Gibbons, a Unitarian Universalist minister and Harvard divinity grad, was acting as our interlocutor with any university personnel that might question our mission. There were 20 of us in all.

Savitri, our director, led the way, peering down hallways, reading signs on the walls, determining our route toward the labs. Susannah Pryce was dressed to the nines as our Queen Bee, in a gold hoopskirt by the French designer Chloé, which we'd found in a vintage shop in the Village. Savitri had outfitted it with a vest and high royal collar, with a hive-like crown on her head. Susannah was a startling image, an African goddess of the honeybees. I was dressed as usual, carrying the cheap bullhorn.

The first scientists we encountered seemed to be too young; they may have been graduate students. Their response from the spacious cafeteria was to stare at us, giggle, and then whip out their iPhone for an Instagram post.

The presence of the bees slows down any defensive response to our invasions — we are not the great unwashed lefty anarchy. Oh, we are grateful for the magic of our body swarms as we march forward. Or maybe that's not quite getting it right. Perhaps we ride the power of the mystical presence of the honey bee. At any rate, it seemed like we got up to the third floor of the Robobee lab before anyone could even open their mouth. People were too busy doing double-takes.

We stationed ourselves opposite a glowing display case, where the sample Robobees were lined up like tiny soldiers. So this would be where the robot drone and our radical Earth bee would square off. The singers lit into our honeybee song, improvising harmonies, singing it again and again. I occasionally boomed through my bullhorn, "THE ROBOBEE DOESN'T MAKE SENSE IN THE ERA OF EXTINCTION," and then finally our quarry — the real scientists — began drifting out into the hallway and into our unusual church service.

I was nervous and zoomed up into the fulminations of an Old Testament preacher, imploring a hands-on prayer on the glass case full of dime-size robots. Reverend Gibbons and Teddy with the camera were moving among the researchers who leaned back against the walls, watching us in a thoughtful daze. They seemed surprised to come out into the hallway, away from their computers, adjusting their eyes to the non-algorithmic light. Some reached over to our basket of almonds and apples, smiling meekly.

No one seemed threatened by these freaks from New York. Instead, the researchers were intrigued. We were a bit confused by this. This wasn't the charged opposition of a Chase bank or a Monsanto lobby. We were deep inside the extreme gentility of ultimate privilege. This was, after all, Harvard, combined with the Department of Defense combined with the romance of pure science.

No, we couldn't possibly threaten these highly paid tinkerers, but could we make them think? We slowly started to talk to each other.

One of the more garrulous drone designers told us, with Teddy T. on the videotape: "People want a story, so what's the story? People are making robots in this building. Very small robots. It's interesting technology, has lots of uses, but what's the story? Need a story for funding, for coverage. So you have to tell a story, so 'Let's not call them robots — let's call them BEES!' That's a good story. Then you call them bees, and Fox News gets upset — 'You're wasting money on bees, what the hell?'"

Well *that* was off the subject. Isn't it more accurate to say that the honeybee *is* your story, because it's dying and you're replacing it? You say in the press that you want to make a mechanical pollinator and then you have nothing to add about Monsanto and Bayer and Syngenta — who are killing the bee and expect to very soon be desperate for a new industrial pollination device for their factory farms? And isn't Fox News just a dead horse, convenient for kicking when you have nothing to say?

I was sensing conversations around me that I'd have loved to stop and enter, but my role as Reverend is to stay in the ethos of the event. We can talk about it later, but while it's happening we're in the heightened state of *Honeybeelujah!* The singers are everywhere, and their harmonies are everywhere. Now they are repeating a simple round that Nehemiah composed in the van coming up on Highway 95: *Oh Robobee — you can't pollinate me / Can't buzz in my hive — my bee is alive!*

Where is Dr. Robert J. Wood, the one conversation we must have? We ask the question from the top of the steps above the second-floor library, where Savitri found a sort of stage for us, and we bunch our individual swarms together into one big swarm with our faces looking out. Where is the young man who financed all this, these labs, this story, this promising weapon, this Robobee? We ask the question, emphasized by the bullhorn, and wait in our swarm.

Our award-winning DARPA scientist is out of town, a writer from the *Harvard Crimson* explains. He knows because he was looking for him too, to get a response to our invasion. Occasionally, as we sing and preach, we see out of the corner of our eye some older people in suits appear; they frown and turn away. The languid scientists keep picking up pollinated produce and then they sneak away to munch in front of their algorithms.

We've paraded all over the building. Unlike the Golden Toads' foray in the Chase bank, we've had no real confrontation in the lab. The one Communications Officer was alarmed that we had the *New Yorker* and Al Jazeera with us in his semi-secret building, and Dr. Woods, our illustrious defendant, was gone at some Pentagon meeting somewhere. And the one scientist who was willing to go on record was framing the whole thing as a marketing problem.

The new story that we must tell might not be based on confrontation. And so it may no longer be a traditional story, with the antagonists, a hero and a villain, the crisis and the resolution at the end. We were singing and shouting in the hallways of that dangerous laboratory with the honeybee's Fabulous Unknown at the heart of our story. The Church of Stop Shopping wanted to talk about the world beyond shopping, the peace beyond bombs, the unknown in the hive. But how do we translate the Earth in a shout?

If we keep trespassing, crossing into power with our whole selves, in full cry, singing and shouting, channeling the Fabulous Unknown — Children! I'm talking about a exhibition of some extreme weather in our hot bodies, amen? — like extinct amphibians spontaneously resurrecting in bank vaults, like grandmothers chained to heavy machinery, like police paralyzed by a siege of visionary survivors, like the returning to life of vanished honeybees and lost artists . . . then we might suddenly have a clear translation when the Earth speaks.

Finally Savitri directed us out of the Robobee Lab. We remembered staying too long at the Chase bank. Anyway, if we stay a half-hour it's an interruption. If we stay an hour it's a bee-in. If we stay until all the crucial conversations we could have here are exhausted, we would be occupying the building.

We sang the honeybee song one final time as we high-stepped, gospel-style, through the door and out into the Wordsworthian sweep of the old campus, and sure enough, bees alighted on our shoulders . . . You think I'm kidding?

SPEAK, EARTH

YOUR WIND MAKES A WHISTLING SOUND in the corner of the apartment, and I know that you are whispering to me, but instead of trying to hear you, I turn on my computer.

I didn't escape you at all. There you are on the screen, an impossible wind with somersaulting cars and flying oil-slicks. You are the Earth rotating inside me like a conscience. These freak storms, tsunamis, droughts and extinctions confirm what I carry inside.

I know that I will have to change some personal consumption in the next few minutes. It might be a light switch, a perfume, a heated pool or a bite of food. But changing can be so tricky. I can change for days and discover I was only spending money.

I know that I am made of the Earth, blood and electricity and bone, and that should make it easier to talk to you. But I turn to words that assure me I am made of something else: titanium, modified molecules, and fifty Super Bowls. In this big box the future looks bright!

I fear the withheld love of a drought. Are you speaking to me? I'm afraid of a dead forest gesturing like a frozen crowd on a mountain. Did you say something?

My neighbors and friends are made of the Earth, too. We share stories about the hurricane, the heat prostration of the elderly woman who used to watch us from the old porch, the storm sewers disgorging poison across the playground. But we have the delete button at the ready. We can quickly move to celebrity gossip, poll numbers, ISIS.

We know you are directing vast articulations toward us, and still we insist on the importance of war. We have a dozen American flags on our street. War is a kind of non-speaking.

I want to defend *you* more than my country, and it makes me sad that this is a choice we face.

I do want to speak to you, though we are so small, so momentary standing here on our street. We are talking in our language. And we have become so casually violent, and have arranged for that violence to take place at a great distance from our manicured personalities. But then we look at the sky. And the dark clouds gather and we know that you will have a word with us now. You are waiting for us. We can feel that you are waiting.

You are here inside how we think and talk in our ordinary day. You rise up through us, in our blood, spinning and singing in our inner ear, like a 500-year downpour. We are startled by what you are saying. Can we handle this? The Earth is much more direct than "the environment."

The climate change is happening in my body and in yours. You are spinning in space and I am supposed to spin with you. I'm so small, down here on my street.

You are speaking to me. You are speaking to us. For our whole history and pre-history, all those millions of spins, we heard you clearly.

We're so small, down here on our street. We're watching. We're not moving. We're not a movement yet, because we've watched so many *End of the World*s. We'll pay to watch the last one.

Do the billions of tiny, naked humans need one more storm? We sense that we're in trouble. So many of us are on the verge of taking that trespassing leap into action. Earthalujah! Maybe we need just one more incredible disaster and then we'll be there.

What's that? Ah, I hear you now: We must make that storm ourselves.

William Talen moved to New York City from San Francisco in the early 1990s, where he had originally created a character that was a hybrid of street preacher, arguably Elvis, and televangelist called Reverend Billy. In New York, Talen began appearing as Reverend Billy on street corners in Times Square, near the recently opened Disney Store. Whereas other street preachers chose Times Square because of its reputation for sin, Reverend Billy's sermons focused on the evils of consumerism and advertising—represented especially by Disney and Mickey Mouse—and on what Talen saw as the loss of neighborhood spirit and cultural authenticity in Rudolph Giuliani's New York.

Talen is the author of various books, including *What Would Jesus Buy?*, which was also the title of Morgan Spurlock's 2007 documentary about Reverend Billy and his mission. Though Talen does not call himself a Christian, he says that Reverend Billy is not entirely a parody of a preacher, and his Church of Stop Shopping has grown to number in the thousands.

The Church of Stop Shopping is a New York City-based community of activists who sing. The Stop Shopping Choir is, as the name suggests, anti-consumerist, and delivers its message with "punk gospel" music on Earth-loving themes.

Savitri D directs the performances in "contested space" as well as on the concert stage. The forty-voice choir and musicians are guided by music director, Nehemiah Luckett. The group's theater presentations in cities across the country include an annual month-long run at Joe's Pub in Manhattan's Public Theater. They recently toured with Neil Young as the opening act in his "Monsanto Years" tour. Their gospel concerts have taken them to mountaintop removal sites, Zuccotti Park, the police station at Ferguson, Missouri, the Temple at Burning Man, Grand Central Station, and traffic jams at the entrance to the Holland Tunnel.

The company has received the OBIE Award, the Alpert Award, the Drama-Logue Award, the Edwin Booth Award, and the Historic Districts Council's Preservation Award (for leading demonstrations to save Manhattan's Poe House). The singers risk arrest together, and were taken into custody recently at the Spectra Pipeline, the Flood Wall Street action, which followed the People's Climate March, at Goldman Sachs near Occupy Wall Street, and in both Ferguson and New York while working with Black Lives Matter. Reverend Billy himself has been arrested over seventy times.